The Story of Infinity

The Story of Infinity

The Collected Works of Gregge Tiffen

P Systems & Associates, Publishers
La Jolla, California

Copyright © 2011 by G-Systems International.
All rights reserved.

The Story of Infinity is published by
P Systems & Associates
P. O. Box 12754
La Jolla, California 92039-2754
www.P-SystemsInc.com • 1-888-658-0668

Without limiting the rights under the copyright reserved above, no part of this publication may be reproduced, stored in or introduced into a retrieval system or transmitted, in any form or by any means (electronic, mechanical, photocopying, recording, or otherwise) without the prior written permission of the copyright owner. The scanning, uploading, and distribution of this book via the Internet or via any other means without the permission of the publisher is illegal and punishable by law. Your support of these rights is appreciated.

Visit www.G-Systems.com or call 1-972-447-9092.

Transcribed by Patrece Powers
Cover design by Lynn Hill

ISBN: 978-0-9842552-9-0

In honor of these mystical storytellers,
whose discipline and dedication provide us with the
keys to how Planet Earth and all its inhabitants are
designed to live and prosper.

These Works of mysticism update that which would otherwise be left behind.

—Gregge Tiffen

Contents

Foreword ix

Introduction 1

Chapter 1: The Code 3

Chapter 2: Before a Beginning 23

Chapter 3: The Basic Elements of Creation 51

Chapter 4: The Construction of Planet Earth 71

Chapter 5: The Mandate 93

Chapter 6: Dominion 111

Chapter 7: Progression 125

Foreword

The Collected Works is a compilation of presentations from Gregge Tiffen's lectures and teachings to which the reader can return beneficially time and time again. Gregge had little time to write due to the sheer magnitude of teaching and lecturing activities that increased year-by-year throughout more than five decades of his work in the field of meta-energy. In addition to his business consultations and lectures, his days were spent meeting the needs of people who sought guidance for personal and professional concerns.

He consistently refused requests to form an organization of any kind in order to insure that his unique training in mysticism, including the Universal Laws of Independence and Individuality, found the proper audience. He felt certain that such teachings must not be confined to the frameworks within organizations. By their very design, organizations develop a hierarchy of personalities that regrettably destroy the atmosphere necessary for the purity to learn and to teach, to lead and to follow.

The style and presentation of materials published in each series of The Collected Works are Gregge's original spoken words. Very little editorial license is taken in order to maintain the clarity and precision that identify how he was taught and, as a result, how he taught. The timeless nature of knowledge precludes indicating times and locations of his teachings. In this way, we are able to support and promote the integrity of Gregge's lifelong dedication to update and correct misinterpretations of ancient wisdoms.

Since all lectures were delivered to audiences familiar with Gregge's mystical training and orientation, we suggest to those who are unacquainted with these principles that you familiarize yourself by reading the *First Encounter Series: Into the Universe* (vol. 1), *Down to Earth* (vol. 2), and *Earth and*

Second Earth (vol. 3). Also, an adventure that you won't want to miss is Gregge's highly acclaimed book, *Life in the World Hereafter: The Journey Continues*. Don't leave earth without it!

Introduction

Esoteric literature is the bastion of mysticism. It is the means by which mystics perpetuate knowledge and the necessary code to keep that knowledge alive. Mysticism, per se, has never been designed for the masses. It is designed for those who have the spiritual desire, willingness, intelligence, and tenacity to understand what it means and what it is meant to do.

True mystical laws (whatever that statement means) are handed from teacher to student and mystic to mystic. Such an approach is supportive enough for the whole field of mysticism. It provides a rather deep insight into what the laws mean, how they work, and how they apply in any number of ways to life itself. You and I are sitting at a point in history in which we have available to us a compendium of material that existed approximately ninety-five hundred years ago.

We can look at the Story of Infinity as an account written approximately four thousand years ago. It was taken from writings that existed about five thousand years before that. This is why you will find a parallel in the Story to almost any other esoteric writings that you want to pick up, no matter what the philosophy might be. I want those readers who are non-Christian not to get upset or have any resistance because we are using the Bible. It happens to be an ideal piece of literature for what we are exploring, so let's get any religious blocks out of the way right away. That way, you can understand the book of Genesis as the Story of Infinity. The Story was not written by a pope, and as a matter of fact, the Old Testament was not written by Christians, nor does it have anything to do with Christianity.

I use the Lamsa translation of the Bible, which comes from the Aramaic of the ancient Peshitta, because I find it to be the best translation. Therefore, we will not be equal word-for-word unless you are using the exact same translation. Nevertheless, whichever translation you are using is going to work out fine as long as it's the Bible and not *Alice in Wonderland*.

The Story of Infinity is not an original. It is plagiarism in its highest and most honorable form. And, I can imagine a time will come in our planetary future (long after we are gone and long after we have even stopped coming) in which this planet will go through certain changes. These changes will likely destroy the literature of historical times, causing it to be replaced by updated literature. That would be nothing more than the continuation of what we left behind mystically and non-mystically.

In esoteric writings, you seldom find one author writing the whole story. Authors change as quickly as paragraphs change, and each author uses his own code language. In mysticism, there are key words that are interchangeable. These words have the same intent, and they mean the same thing. For instance, *God, devil* and *spirit*, were interchangeable terms at the time the Bible was written. The authors had the same intent, which makes this very confusing until you understand the author's code.

It is in the first chapter of Genesis that we find the keys to how Planet Earth is designed to operate. The first chapter, in particular, is nothing more than a recapitulation of earlier material that has been around in one form or another since this planet began. The laws of this planet are all here.

Now, let's get started with the Story because it is most interesting and very exciting.

ONE

The Code

God created the heavens and the earth in the very beginning.
                                                     Genesis 1:1

We have some very interesting words coming out of this first sentence. Doesn't it strike you as rather overwhelming that, just like that, in the first line of the book there is an identification of a Supreme Being without any preface to the Supreme Being? You are told that this is "the most important book in the world" (if you go by print sales), but then the first thing you come across is *God created*. You've got to stop. The first thing to realize is that a great deal of information is being translated into a workable language for communication.

One of the key factors in the literary use of mysticism is to question. If you don't, you're going to miss the essence of the whole meaning. This leaves you in a state of having an unanswerable beginning, and you are really thrown out to sea. You have to question: Who is this? What is this? Why is it so? Being mystics (as they were) and writing the Story, they just assumed that other mystics knew what the preface was to their piece of work. Their term for *God* has something to do with a Supreme Being who was referred to in preceding works. Picking up the Story as a normal human being, you are left in the cold when you read *God created*. If you don't know, you read it and begin to accept what you read. People do this all the time. They say, "Well, of course, we know who God is." It is just such acceptance without questioning that is wrong.

How could you start a story with the first sentence as, "Gregge created chaos"? What publisher would buy such a manuscript? Who the hell is this guy? You have to build a character. You have to know who "he" is. However, here you pick up the most important writing that has affected the world in the last three or four thousand years, and it starts out with *God created*. Right there, in terms of the writing, when you run into a situation where a character is there, who is not established, something must have preceded it. The point I am making is that if a preface isn't there, you have to realize that it's somewhere else.

Beginning is another word we have to take a look at, following this unexplainable God. We are trying to find out the most important thing in our lives. How is this planet on which we find ourselves supposed to operate? And, at the very beginning of this rule book, we are thrown into such disarray that we aren't even sure if we can go on with the reading, much less with the understanding. We don't have any answers. We don't know who *God* is, and we don't know what *created* means. What is what? What does the word *created* mean? How did God create, and who was it who did it? We have a whole pot filled with these questions.

In terms of learning, this goes on in mysticism all of the time. If you avoid trying to find out the who, the what, the why, the when, and the where, then you aren't worthy of the study. What if I, Gregge Tiffen, had sat in front of my old teacher when he had said, "Alright, read me the first line."? And I read aloud, "God created the heavens and the earth in the very beginning," and then I just sat there. I think he would have put me out in the snow for seventeen months while I thought about it. This is very important because the first thing you have to learn as you go through any kind of philosophical writing is not to accept what is stated just because it is stated. You must ask, what is going on? What is the writer is saying. Am I supposed to know this? Am I supposed to accept this? If there isn't a preface, I better go dig one up.

What you need to do, in terms of this first line, is to put the Story down and walk away. Go find the answers to these basic questions because there isn't any sense in going any further. You don't have an answer, and the writer didn't give you an answer, so you're back to the basic proof that the Story is an update of previous writings. There is a stated assumption here. The assumption is that you automatically know that the writing is taken from something else. You would know this, if you were a mystical student.

All of this works if the writer is correct in assuming that you know who *God* is, that you know what *created* means, and that you know what *heavens* and *earth* mean. The writer, who is a mystic, has a reference, and he expects the writings to be read by mystics who also have the reference. He just assumes that you know the reference as well. Nevertheless, there are millions of people who pick up the Story, read it, and go on without one iota of intelligent understanding relative to its meaning. I want you to recognize that what we have here is a code book. You receive a first-time experience, which is first-time awareness.

You will see, as we go along, that mystical writings are laid out for you in such a way that they absolutely obliterate your ability to include any of your references. The writings are so accurate that the only reference is to that of the writer and never to your reference. The mystic literally snatches your mind away from you and holds it in the palm of his hand. He says, "I mold it in the way that I want to mold it, and if you don't understand it this way, you'll never understand what I am doing." You might find the meaning of the word, but you still won't necessarily know the intended meaning of the author. In some cases he'll allow you to refer back, and in some cases he'll set in his own code. You'll see all of this come out as we go along. What we're doing is investigating the concept of the writer.

Every mystic worth his candle and incense knows that there never was a beginning. Yet, the very first line of the most important writing says, *God created the heavens and the earth in the very beginning.* As the reader of this code, what are you going to do when you come up against a line like this? You don't know who *God* is. You don't know how He *created*. You don't know the definition of *heavens* and *earth*, and it all happened *in the very beginning.* If you don't know one factor, you can't begin to know one of the other factors. Since one factor is a non-established quantity and quality, what follows is also a non-established quantity and quality.

The whole opening line of Genesis is to destroy your ability to understand what has been written, and this is done for a reason. Again, the reason is that the Story is written by mystics for mystics. The uninitiated reader picks up Genesis and reads, *God created the heavens and the earth in the very beginning*. Then the uninitiated says, "Ah-ha, let's go on from there."

That's when the mystic says, "Great, if you don't stop at that point, everything else you read is going to be worthless to you, and that's exactly what I intended. I'm not giving you the code. I'm giving it to those who know or to those who are trying to learn and only to those people." Don't you see the whole wonderful essence of this? It's as if the mystical writer has taken a very valuable piece of gold and painted it black. You pick it up, throw it down, and you walk off. You think it's just a piece of iron. That is exactly what the mystic wants you to do with this first sentence. He wants you to pick it up and, without seeing that he has referenced the infinity of knowledge, put it down because you don't know who or what *God* is, or what *created* and *beginning* mean. You don't know what these terms are because none of them are explicable. This is because they don't really exist. God doesn't really exist. Creation doesn't really exist. Beginning doesn't really exist.

If there is nothing else that shows you the intricacies of this kind of literature, this line will do it. The writer assumes that if you know, you have the key to move on. If you don't know, you're going to toss it away as worthless iron. Right there, he's got you by the proverbial spiritual throat. You either come up with an answer, or you don't. It is just so beautiful. Right off the bat, this separates the learner from the non-learner and the ignorant from the intelligent. The beauty of it always overwhelms me because of the innuendos and the intricacies of constructing such an enormously important line and then covering it up. It's as if he's saying, "The wise man will scratch it and know it is gold, and the ignorant will throw it away." It's a tremendous piece of work right there. This is not the book of Genesis. It is the book of Infinity. It is a story that has no beginning, and a story that has no end.

You can say, "Oh yes, I know what the writer means. I know that God created the heavens and the earth in the very beginning." If you approach people and ask them if they know what this line means, they are likely to say, "Absolutely." They might spend seven hours telling you how God created the heavens and the earth in the very beginning, and not one whit of it is correct because none of it can be explained. When you read mystical writings, you have to be able to let go of those things that you normally use for association. When you say "God," you have an impression, but you have to get rid of that impression because that kind of thing does not exist anyplace. We don't have a God in those terms. We don't have the slightest idea of what creation is. We stand by as observers and watch creation take place, but we don't know what it is. Scientists work very hard at trying to find out what creation is as they investigate the building blocks of DNA and RNA, thinking maybe they can reproduce it, but they still don't know.

Any intelligent individual will be the first to admit that the beginning of anything cannot be found because everything seems to be related to something that preceded it. An event is just an event. It is not the beginning of anything. We can see a series of events interlocked by a series of will actions. It's a chain of events. For instance, you can go back fifty thousand years, but you're not really interested in fifty thousand years of history. You now have more current events of interest.

The operating Law of Infinity at this point of creation is that nothing is really divided. Do divisions exist? If I have a line and that line has a plus polarity and a minus polarity, where does the plus polarity leave off and the minus polarity begin? Don't you see what's wrong? The whole sentence, *God created the heavens and the earth in the very beginning*, is a sentence of nothing. *God* is singular, *created* is singular, *beginning* is singular, but *the heavens and the earth* is a division. It is a sentence of infinity. You cannot divide the heavens and the earth because there are no divisions in the Universe. There is no God. There is no creation. There are no beginnings, and there are no divisions. The whole line throws us right back into the very essence of what the writer is establishing. The whole code book is the operating Law of Infinity at this point of creation on Planet Earth.

Nothing is really divided. In the United States, our forefathers established the idea, "Out of many, one" (i.e., *e pluribus unum*). United we stand. Divided we fall. This is a very esoteric statement. If you were to have division, you would have an anti-universal condition, and nothing stands divided in the Universe because there's no possible division in the Universe. As a matter of fact, the people who drew up the Constitution of the United States were mostly Masons. They were very well-versed in mysticism. The seal on the dollar bill and other symbols were all purposefully used for mystical means.

It is an outrage, in terms of the masses, that we have allowed fakery to be perpetrated upon us and to beat us down as a workable society, a workable humanity, and a progressive planet. This material that was originally written by mystics for mystics eventually got into the hands of the masses. It was translated for the masses and then used to establish a law, a canon, or a dogma. It was then interpreted to enslave a church congregation (whatever "church" might mean but not necessarily the Christian church) for the purpose of an organization. It was not done philosophically. It was done deliberately to enslave people.

This was done a long time ago, and I am not blaming the current church administrators. I am turning to those individuals who started it, despite knowing what the interpretation should be, and who deliberately interpreted differently in order to enslave. You need to understand that the early Christian churches were chaotic. They were constantly overrun with internal strife and power struggles. I'm talking about the churches in 40 and 50 A.D. and in those earlier years. Paul spent all of his time trying to get the people to stop fighting. Everyone was trying to position themselves to be the top dog. His letters to the churches were pleas to quit fighting among themselves and get down to the business of what was then Christianity. The churches, as they progressed, were the great landlords of Europe around 900 to 1100 A.D. They owned slaves and feudal properties. The bishops went to war against one another. The Bible bound everyone to those who purposefully misinterpreted the writings. I have to defend the mystical writers. They had no intention of the writings falling into the hands of those who would do this. And, to this day, the Bible still remains a code.

I don't expect you to spend time with this material and say, "This is the right way" any more than I expect you to do that with anything else. At the very least, it will give you some ability to reach your own decisions, and you will be a better person for whatever decisions you reach.

Let's get back to the essence of infinity and the very subtle and beautiful ways in which the mystical writer asks whether you understand. If you do, please go on. If you do not understand, the mystic is safe because you will not understand anything else that follows, and he will not be misinterpreted. You are meant to assume that you are reading the Story of Infinity, the Laws of Infinity, and the application of the laws. This is a very fine assumption since that's the exact intention of the mystical writers who make use of every single word. They do this emphatically, dramatically, and so intensely that you cannot afford to speed-read because you would miss the importance.

And the earth was without form, and void;

Genesis 1:2[*]

We must always look at connector words. When we read, *And the earth was without form, and void,* it shows that there is a

---

[*] In the Lamsa translation, there is a comma after *form* and a semicolon after *void*.

continuation of thought. Nothing has stopped. You will see more in the meaning of this as we explore other connectors besides the word *and*. The writer is showing you a definite flow action that he wants you to understand. Whether there's a period there or not, he is taking you onward and telling you that this action flows. This gives you a very important picture in terms of the Universe: that the planet is established as a natural continuation. It is the natural progression of the Universe in Its infinity. The writer is saying, "Look, you must see this as a continuum and not as bits and pieces here and bits and pieces there." The whole thing works out of natural progression in universal form. That *and* is terribly, terribly important.

This second sentence should immediately confuse you. Look at the first line: *God created the heavens and the earth in the very beginning*. Then look at the juxtaposition between that line and this second line: *And the earth was without form, and void*. Our definition of creation is really manifestation. You can't create without manifesting on this planet, so if you create and you create the earth, there's a manifested form. However, the writer goes on to tell you in the next line that there isn't any form. At this particular point, you can sit around and say, "What in the hell is going on here?" It's as if two different people are writing two different stories and trying to put the sentences together without any thought to the meaning.

And the earth was without form, and void; What is the meaning of *void*? *Void* is a contradiction. There is no point in the universe that has a void or a vacuum. That is just irrationally stated and impossible, so what does this mean in terms of esoteric logic? The first verse tells us—by the way it's written—that this whole story is about Infinity. For example, *God* and *created* are mentioned. *The heavens and the earth* (which indicate a division) and *the beginning* do not exist as we know them. They exist only in the universal sense, which is an infinite sense. We need to say to ourselves, "This cannot be, since *created* has to have a form to manifest. If it were manifest, there could not be a void because a void is a place where nothing exists." We now realize this means nothing.

We are meant to understand that these words are coded. The mystical writer is trying to give us a statement of something by not stating the something he is trying to tell us. He does this by stating something that is so impossible and so intangible that we cannot accept it literally. We must reject the statement literally in order to find out what it means beyond all sense and all thought as we know it.

And the earth was without form, and void; must mean that the point where the earth was established was pre-established in consciousness before manifestation and before the actual planet mass was put at this point. Don't you see? In actuality, manifestation had to be pre-planned in consciousness. It had to be pre-thought by First Cause of Mind, the Infinite Thinker. Pre-planning had to take place before the planet could be established in the solar system. There was space but not empty space. There was just no mass there. There is no empty space anywhere in the Universe.

In order for the planet to be established in the solar system, some planning in Supreme Consciousness had to take place. The mystical writer is telling you that it was no accident that the planet was formed in this space; it was pre-planned. How do we know it was pre-planned? Because the writer writes in such a way that nothing can be taken literally. All of this is held at great depth to make you reach for it, in-depth, because he wants the student to go in and find the meaning and to be at that level of intelligence. Why? It's very simple. When you attain the level of intelligence at which you willingly probe for the meaning, you're then at the level of intelligence at which you will understand. Until such time, you couldn't possibly understand anyway. If you can't understand, that is information that cannot be used, and in an all-Intelligent, omnipotent Universe, waste is not allowed.

Can you see the lovely subtleties that the mystical writer uses in this particular way? You read: *And the earth was without form, and void.* Nothing was established because it had to be pre-planned. It had to come out of the law and order of major consciousness or Supreme Consciousness, if you like. Nothing in the Universe happens by accident. Nothing just explodes, and there it is. Everything is done according to law and order. The position of this planet wasn't conceived by any roll of the dice. Creation has its law and order and a place for everything. Right there is a very important aspect of the law that affects you. If this planet has been pre-conceived, and pre-conceived to be in the right place at the right time, then you are pre-conceived, and your position here is equally as planned in a universal sense.

You have got to automatically assume that you are pre-conceived and that your position here is equally as planned, as important, and as right as the planet itself. An inconceivable individual would not be put on a conceivable planet. Right there, the Universe would destroy Itself with that kind of inconsistency. Your position here is assured to be correct because the planet is correct to begin with and conceived out of Prime Consciousness.

And the earth was without form, and void; and darkness was upon the face of the deep.

Genesis 1:2

There are two key words here. What is *darkness*? Is the writer talking about the lack of light, or is he talking about something else? Do not put down *darkness* as being negative. We have the human habit of using *darkness* to mean "lesser than light," and many times, writers do use *darkness* to mean "lesser than light." However, we're at the very early stages of this writing, so we don't want to presume that kind of idea until we're sure.

Let's see what we have here: *and darkness was upon the face of the deep.* Is the writer talking about a lack of light, or is he talking about something else? The word *light* has not been introduced yet, so we can't presume *darkness* is the polarity of light—yet. The writer has us trapped on purpose because he doesn't intend *darkness* to be the polarity of light in this context. Consider the preceding line and verse: *And the earth was without form, and void;*

Now we have, *and darkness was upon the face of the deep.* The point in the universe for the birth of the planet has been picked out by Supreme Consciousness. The writer goes on to say that *darkness was upon the face of the deep.* In other words, *darkness* (in this case) does not mean "the absence of light." It means "receptivity," in the same sense as the womb of a female is dark inside. It is a dark, receptive place of birth, and used here, *darkness* indicates a place to give birth and a place to receive because the sentence goes on to say, *darkness was upon the face of the deep.* We are told that the space is being prepared.

Supreme Consciousness determined that the planet would exist. Supreme Consciousness determined that the planet would exist at this point in the universe, and Supreme Consciousness pre-established this point for the birth of the planet. This is the same way that a female prepares in terms of pregnancy to harbor, receive, and accept the seed in the womb. The writer is drawing you a very, very clear picture. Up to now he is saying, "I am telling you the Story of Infinity, my children." He goes on to say, "Long before anyone can remember, Divine Consciousness determined that a planet would be born at this point in space. Divine Consciousness then prepared the space for the planet." That's all that he has told you up to now, but he has told you volumes. In five lines, the mystic has told you more than people tell you in books, books, and more books.

Don't automatically assume that one word is the polarity to another word. The mystical writer tells you only what he wants to tell you. Don't read anything <u>into</u> what he tells you. Read <u>what</u> he tells you, and find out if it computes. If it doesn't compute, you know immediately that he wants you to find out what he means by looking into the opposite condition, not the opposite word. He's not using the opposite word. *And the earth was without form, and void; and darkness was upon the face of the deep.* Period.

And the Spirit of God moved upon the face of the water.

Genesis 1:2

Here we go again. All of sudden, he's thrown something new right smack-dab in the middle of the second verse. He starts out with *and* to indicate that there is no separation in carrying the story through; therefore, we know it's connected to the preceding intent. What in the world are we going to do with, *And the Spirit of God*? We haven't even defined *God*, which starts the story off, but now he's talking about the spirit of God. What is the spirit of anything? We must stop and wonder. First, we were told that *God created the heavens and the earth*, but then the writer uses, *And the Spirit of God*. Perhaps we were right in initially assuming that there was no such thing as God, since it's the spirit—the essence—of God that makes something work. When we talk about the essence of anything, we aren't talking about something that has manifested. We're talking about the part that we assume is there because we're observing the character of the thing. From that assumption, we say that the essence is "such and such." We may be right. By taking away the definition as an identifiable being or action of God, the mystical writer begins to give us the first inkling of what God is. He is talking about the essence or the spirit of God. This is very, very important. He's trying to get us to understand that it is not God who creates, but that it's the essence of God that creates. We don't know what the essence of God is, but we can assume by observation. If I were to pose the question to forty people, "What is God?," I'd get forty different answers. I doubt that even two answers would be remotely alike. Now, we're getting some idea of the infinity of First Cause that started the whole Story of Infinity.

The mystical writer is doing something to protect himself, to keep away from those who lack the understanding when he writes, *And the Spirit of God moved upon the face of the water*. A brand new term is introduced. *Water* used in any form is spiritual. The mystic uses it over and over again to explain a state of spiritual being whether he's talking about a sea, a waterfall, a stream, or water in a glass. Water is always the symbol of spirituality. In the New Testament of the Bible, we read that Jesus walked upon the water and he went to the well where the Good Samaritan gave him a drink of water. In the Old Testament, Moses parted the sea. Water keeps showing up as the symbol of spirituality. The student who understands symbolism also understands that water is spirituality.

Now we go back to *And the Spirit of God* [which is the essence of God that we cannot see or define] *moved upon the face of the water*. The essence moved upon the face of spirituality. What is the face of spirituality as proposed in the sentence, *And the Spirit of God moved upon the face of the water*? If the meaning is overlooked, you miss the whole essence of the law. That's how important it is. What is happening? We are talking about a point in space that's prepared for the birth of this planet. *And the Spirit of God moved upon the face of the water*, not *the face of the deep*, but *moved upon the face of the water*. We have a different space involved here. There is no manifestation at this point in space. We have already learned that water is always the symbol of spirituality. At this point, there isn't any manifestation. There is no real water in spirituality, so what can it possibly mean when the *Spirit of God moved upon the face of the water*? We have to look at the essence of the elements that we're dealing with here. If I move anything across that kind of a surface, I'm talking about a reflection. We do not have a planet yet. This is the essence of God seeing His reflection at this point in space. The author is telling us that this is the continuity to the preamble for the birth of the planet.

The point in space was chosen accurately and made ready to receive, and the next step was God showing His reflection of His spirituality at that point. We now know, in effect, what the sperm of the Universe was for the birth of this planet. It was intercourse, if you like, between Divine Consciousness and that point in space getting ready for the beginning of the planet. The writer is telling you in his own code (which he has a right to do) what he wants to tell you. It must make sense. If we have space and we have water but neither one of them really exists, what is the only thing that could really exist? When you look in the mirror, what really exists? What transpires between the mirror and you? There is a transmission of molecular movement between two points that you cannot see in its raw form, but you may see the movement as color, shape, and form as your eyes make the registration in reflection.

Carry that picture of reflection to this point in space where nothing existed. The essence of God finds a reflection on a point of water that does not exist. What could possibly be taking place? The only thing that could take place is an image because nothing else is there. An image is nothing more than the transaction of energy from point A to point B, where nothing is happening in between except the recognition of one of those two points. When working in concert with the planet, we have a lot of information here on how to create.

Translate this into your own life terms. As your essence moves upon your spirituality (the image itself), the place is fully prepared. The writer is talking about preparing the place before you reflect or begin imaging. In modern mind science, the metaphysician thinks that all you have to do is to begin imaging. He doesn't prepare the place. He doesn't really get down to the fact that you must pre-plan and decide where the thing should go and accurately work out the details in order to put the thing where it belongs. The proper preparation is awareness.

And the Spirit of God [the essence] *moved upon the face of the water.* There is no definition yet for *God*, but we will get to it. The writer knows that God, creation, and beginning are not explainable. He wants you to recognize that the story he is telling you is the story of a continuation of other information that existed. It is a story that's unexplainable just as infinity is unexplainable. He is giving you the best picture he knows. Later on, he becomes very definitive. However, at that point, it almost blows your mind. You then realize that you've been led to believe one thing, and all of a sudden, a whole new picture appears.

The writer is telling you, "Look, there's no way that I can tell you where this all began." What you need to understand is that there is a standard for the way we do things on this planet. Some God-essence impregnates a point in space when that point is ready. When the female is fertile, she can become pregnant, but she cannot become pregnant if she isn't fertile. In other words, there has to be a biological preparation within the female. Acting as the feminine polarity here, space has to be fertile. It has to be ready to accept the impregnation. Where does the impregnation come from? It comes from the essence of God in terms of spirituality. What is spirituality? We don't know because we don't know what spirit is. We don't know what essence is either, but we do know that essence has enough power to impregnate this point in space. When that point has been established in Supreme Consciousness, the space is then prepared for the birth of the planet. It's all very logical.

This gives you the whole key as to how the planet was set up. It didn't just fly off indiscriminately from the sun and start whirling around by some gravitational pull. There was more to all of this. In much of what he writes, the mystic is telling you that there's a whole continuum of deep esoteric, scientific thought from which he sometimes gives you mathematical equations and sometimes philosophical equations. There is always tremendous depth required to understand that which is basically not understandable. In effect, he's saying that he doesn't care what astronomers might say in terms of how the planet was born. He's telling us that the planet was born out of very deeply aware Supreme Consciousness that prepared for it, impregnated the space, and allowed for it all to happen according to a plan.

One of the first things we learn out of the Story of Infinity is that things are working according to law and order. Everything follows a pattern, and that is very important. It means that, since the earth followed a pattern, everything on the planet is also going to follow a pattern into its being.

When a seed hits the ground, the ground is always prepared and receptive to those things that can grow. The nature of the ground is to accept those things that can grow in the soil. The seed becomes the impregnator, and something grows. Without the seed, the ground is not impregnated; it is just receptive. The point is simply that many things we don't think are receptive to growth are basically receptive to growth. The earth is always receptive. In light of what the writer is telling us, receptivity requires preparation. Everything has to be prepared. Then, we are ready for action.

And God said,

Genesis 1:3

The key here is that the first thing that established the planet was sound. The first basic precept of the earth's personality is in sound. If sound established the planet, we might say that, after the place in space was prepared for the planet, there was an enormous explosion. This explosion caused a sound to occur of such magnitude that it's beyond anything we can conceive. The point is that the planet was established in sound. Therefore, anything you want to do on this planet must follow the precept of sound. You can have the world's greatest idea, but until it's put forward in sound, it means nothing. You can write the most unbelievably intelligent book that mankind has ever seen, but if it's just read and never spoken about, it means nothing. It's only when someone takes what you have written and puts it into some kind of sound that it becomes alive and manifests itself on the planet.

You can think that you know all there is to know about all there is to know, but as long as that remains up in your head and you never utter a word about what you know, you have learned nothing. You have done nothing, and you have manifested nothing. This is why the most beautiful things are those things you experience through sound: the voice of someone you love, the whisper of something you just faintly hear, the waves up against the shoreline, music, ad infinitum.

Whatever it may be, nothing makes a deeper impression on us than sound.

The writer has now given us another step of great enormity. In the Story of Infinity, he tells us of a place in space having been prepared. He tells us of the space having been prepared in spirituality by the essence of God's image being reflected. He tells us that the actual birth of the planet occurred in sound. There is a great parallel to this in our human lives. The first sound a baby makes when born is a cry. Sound brings life with it as the initiator of that life. In fact, doctors become very concerned if they slap a baby and the baby breathes without a sound issuing forth. The doctor expects, from the natural function of clearing the lungs, that the baby will cry. Sound is the very initiator of life and brings life with it.

A thought as a thought is wisdom unmanifested. Suppose I wrote a short story, and I gave it to you. And you said nothing. Then, you gave it to someone else who said nothing. Over a period of time, it was passed around, and no one said anything. You wouldn't know what anyone was thinking about your short story until someone said something about what they think or feel. The point is that, without sound, nothing comes alive. Whatever it is does nothing but wait for birth. Manifestation on this planet must come from some sort of sound.

For example, in other discussions and at other points in your life, this information will seep through. While you may not directly quote from the story, you'll paraphrase and integrate this information into your own thinking and conversations. The knowledge comes out and is born within you. It was born in me when I told it to you. It is born in you when you use it in your own right from that point on.

If I read something that's interesting or very striking to me, I will verbalize right then and there. I will talk to myself out loud. I might say, "Isn't that interesting!" Or, I might commend it. Just doing this brings it alive for me. You know this to be true when you read something of an interesting or profound nature. The first logical act is to immediately verbalize it to someone else in some way.

And God said does not indicate anything regarding the use of words. Sound manifested. Period. I might have a great idea and I say, "Aha!" You ask me what that was for and I then say, "None of your business." It does not make any difference. I've manifested out of my head into sound with the "Aha!" It's alive because it issued forth from my mind into actuality. It now exists as a manifested idea. It probably needs more words to see it in concrete form, but it's alive. On the other hand, if you ask what I'm doing, and I reply, "I'm thinking," and you then ask what am I thinking about and I say nothing in response, I have just built up a lot of frustration, if nothing else. At that point, I am in a stagnant space. The Law of Manifestation says I must manifest by sound.

Let's go back to *And God said*. Right there, in the first three words of the second verse, is the first major Law of Planet Earth. All things—to be in existence—must manifest through the use of sound. There's no way of getting around it. You cannot bend this phrase into anything but what it is. The first viable, readable, identifiable manifestation for the planet was sound. It could have been an explosion, but it was sound, and sound will occur under any number of conditions.

For example, the loudest sound I know of on the planet is a tree growing. Can you hear it? You can clairaudiently, and if you know how to do it clairaudiently, you have never heard such a roar. I'm referring to any sound, not just what drifts into my ear atmospherically. I have not heard anything, including the noise on battlefields, louder than a large tree growing. You don't hear it, and maybe I don't hear it with my human ears, but it is there. It is growing, and it is making a sound. The tree is fulfilling the first Law of Manifestation. Grass also makes a sound when it grows.

Thought makes sound in terms of electrical impulses, just as the electricity that goes through your body makes an enormous racket. However, we get to a touchy point here. If thought makes sound through electrical impulse, then does it cause manifestation? This is a very technical point. Technically, the answer is yes. Some telepathy makes sound, and some does not. It depends on what you are doing, who is the sender, who is the receiver, and where it is being done. However, in talking about the Law of Manifestation on Planet Earth and what the author intends for us to understand, the answer is no. When he writes *And God said*, he is really telling us that the planet is manifested by sound. The first law we must understand is to express in sound. This can be words, it can be music, or it can be any combination of things.

And God said. We now know that Planet Earth is a planet manifested by sound.

Discussion Questions

Can you identify having had a first-time experience?

What does the term *God* reference?

How can there be a beginning if everything is related to what preceded it?

Are there divisions in an infinite Universe?

What was in this space before Planet Earth formed and manifested?

In the mystical code, what does *water* mean?

In the mystical code, what does *essence* mean?

What do you need to do before taking any kind of action?

What is a thought?

What is the first basic precept of the earth's personality — the First Prime Law of Manifestation?

Two

Before a Beginning

And God said, Let there be light; and there was light.

Genesis 1:3

We have learned that *And God <u>said</u>* indicates that the first Prime Law of Manifestation on this planet is sound. Next, we come to:

And God said, Let there be light; and there was light.

Genesis 1:3

We first learned that *darkness* meant "receptivity" and (at this point in the story) had nothing to do with being the polarity to light. It meant "receptivity." We now find polarity in the word *light*. We need to stop right here. The mystical writer doesn't want us to relate to just the things we know. Possibly, he's trying to teach you something that you don't know. He has already established darkness as a state of receptivity and not as a polarity to light. He has also established that the place was pre-established in space for the birth of the planet. *And God <u>said</u>* is most likely the explosion that occurred for the birth of this planet. It may have been a roar, but whatever it was, there was sound. The planet was born right then and there. *And God said* signifies the birth of this planet.

Since we know that *darkness* is used by this mystic as his own code to indicate receptivity, then *Let there be light* must be the first <u>action</u> to issue forth the planet as a being. Sound developed the planet and was immediately followed by the planet's own energy from receptivity to activity. We are now given the polarities of darkness and light as receptivity and activity. To carry this even further, darkness equals ignorance and light equals knowledge. This is the same as darkness equals receptivity and light equals activity. We are now considering polarities between the two but not as male and female energy since humanity has not even come upon the scene yet.

What we do have at this particular point is consciousness on the universal level or God-level, if you prefer. The reflection of the essence of God, *the Spirit of God*, is the spirituality in which the planet is couched. Sound has been established as the first manifesting force and immediately following the sound is this planet's initial first activity. To get a better picture of this, consider when the baby is issued forth and taken from its mother. The umbilical chord is cut; the baby is turned upside-down and slapped. The baby then cries. From that point on, who is responsible for the energy function of the baby? The baby is. The baby's physical vehicle is functioning with its spirit on its own accord. The first sound is followed immediately by the issuing forth of the baby's own energy. If you could hear the sound at the micro millisecond when consciousness enters the physical vehicle, you would probably hear an enormous thud. That's the activation of the electrical energy of the body established by the orientation of the consciousness and its energy entering into the physical vehicle, the baby's body. Likewise, the earth is born in sound and issues forth from that point on with its own energy. In other words, *Let there be light* [activity] *and there was light* [activity].

And God said, Let there be light [activity] *and there was light* [activity]. Once again, we have the word *and* as a connector to indicate continuity, but let's not miss that there was an order given, a direction, that said, *Let there be light*. The second Prime Law of Manifestation for this planet is that it's a planet that operates by direction. The first Prime Law of Manifestation is that the planet manifests on the basis of sound, and now the second Prime Law of Manifestation for this planet is that it operates by direction. In order for energy to manifest, we must direct the energy.

The phrase *Let there be light; and there was light* is extremely important. The mystical writer first tells you that, "Here is the Story of Infinity, of which I can tell you nothing peculiar, but I will tell you how I know that it works." His second statement tells you that there was this point in space where a place was prepared for the birth of the planet. The planet manifested itself in sound and issued forth. In doing this, it immediately established its own energy. There was nothing that could be done to stop the manifestation and issuing forth because continuity (the furtherance of energy furthering itself moving inexorably onward) is universal. *And God said, Let there be light; and there was light.* It's as if God gave direction for something that He knew was going to happen anyway.

Can you begin to see how *and* works as a connector to indicate continuity? By using the word *and* in his writings, the writer continues warning you that everything is going to be a process of continuity. There is no way that there's going to be a stoppage to this particular development. It's as if the writer is standing back and saying, "Here's what is happening out there, folks." He is giving you a run-down of what's happening: *and* this is happening, *and* that is happening. He's not saying, "I think I will stop and hold that aside." He continues to give you a whole sequential picture.

And God said, Let there be light was the natural observation of the continuation of the flow, and then of course, *there was light*. Once you see point A and you observe its continuity to point B and you observe point B's continuity to point C, the logical direction to go is point D. This is important to you in practical terms. You do not change your life by tangents. If you're going to use the universal laws that are set up for this planet, then you are going to make a valid observation of these particular points, but you aren't necessarily going back to correct anything. When you say, "I want to straighten myself out," you don't go from point D to point N. You can't go off on a right angle like that. You say, "If I am at point D and this is my point of awareness, then *let it be*, let it happen." What's going to happen? Your next logical step from point D has to be point E. You may want to get to point N, but you're only going to get to point N by going through points E, F, G, H, I, J, K, L, and M, taking it step-by-step-by-step. You don't take quantum leaps because nothing on this earth works that way. You see where you have gone. Autumn comes along. You don't have one day of summer and the next day of autumn.

Watch nature, and you will see how nature uses the law. There are very gradual and definitive transitions. A leaf changes its color a shade at a time. It finally falls off the tree. When springtime comes, the bud appears. At first, it is so small that your eye doesn't even notice it, but eventually the blossom and the leaves appear. Before you know it, the tree is in full bloom. Look at all those moment-by-moment and day-by-day transitions in your own life. This is just like saying, *Let there be,* and there it was because that's the absolute and natural universal progression for this planet. Nothing can stop energy! You can try getting in the way, holding up your hand, and thinking you can stop it, but you're never going to stop the action of energy.

The establishment of the planet at its spiritual level is the continuation of will. The exercise of will occurs at the point of impregnation when God (or the Universe, if you prefer) <u>saw</u> the spiritual image of Himself. Refer to the line: *And the Spirit of God moved upon the face of the water.* That was the last step of will. The planet had not been born yet. It was like pulling the switch, and no matter what you wanted to do from there on, the energy was going to flow. All the preparation was the organization leading up to the event, which ended at the point where it is written: *And the earth was without form, and void; and darkness was upon the face of the deep.* That indicates the point in space picked out for the earth to be birthed, which constitutes the event as seen in the next line: *And the Spirit of God <u>moved</u> upon the face of the water.* At that particular point, the event ended, and will had taken place. *The Spirit of God <u>moved</u>.* In other words, the essence of God took an action. In effect, when the essence of God moved, the Universe was taking the action of will, of determining a direction. The

Universe holds the ultimate option to will. Let's say that I have this enormous blackboard and this is where I am going to start writing on it. Up to this particular point I have pointed to the blackboard, but I haven't made a mark. I've just chosen the specific place. When I decide to write, it is now will. If I pull my hand back without making a mark, you will immediately lose the point that I had pointed to because there's nothing there.

And God saw that the light was good; and God separated the light from the darkness.

Genesis 1:4

Once again, *And* lets us know that we are still in the same story. The writer continues reporting about what's going on. However, we have a brand new word, *saw*, with a brand new meaning. *And God saw.* We understood *God said,* and we took that to mean that the earth was manifested in sound, the first Prime Law of Manifestation. Now, we read *God saw,* so before we get to the word *good,* let's consider *And God saw.*

We found out that God didn't say anything, but rather, there was a sound that took place on a universal level. Now, we find out that God *saw.* We can't transfer *saw* back to an individualized point. This is not an individualized point that we can see. So, what are we dealing with at this point? We are dealing with reflection. *And God saw that the light was good. God* didn't *see* anything. Reflection is being used to indicate seeing. Here comes the third Prime Law of Manifestation.

The third Prime Law of Manifestation for this planet is that the planet's manifestation occurs only by reflection. What drives you up the wall here are two things. First, it's hard enough to think that the only reason you and I exist is by reflection. Second, there is a good possibility in theoretical mysticism that the planet does not even exist. It's possible that Planet Earth is a point in space that is nothing more than universal reflection. We could spend years and years exploring that one. The earth might exist, but we are not too sure.

Up to this point, we have three Prime Laws of Manifestation, and none of those laws is a detriment to or an argument against any of the other two laws. They are all in the natural progression to one another. Because we have to communicate, we say that the planet came into manifestation by sound. We immediately know that the energy must be directed in order to operate and that we are doing our job when we direct energy. Now, we are taking one step further. That which we see manifested is a reflection. What does a manifestation reflect? Manifestation is a reflection of you. For example, you paint a picture. The picture is a reflection of your thought coming through you onto the painting. Everything you do is a reflection of you. If you truly do not see evil, then it doesn't exist as your reflection.

This gets very involved. You may need to work with the negative and not see it as a negative. What this amounts to is that your life has to be predicated upon these laws if you are to live harmoniously on Planet Earth at this point in the universe. In the third Prime Law of Manifestation for this planet, you must realize that everything you see is a reflection of you, whether you determine it to be good or bad. I don't know that you can turn away from this. When you look at someone and find something that is distasteful (which you can do with just about anyone you see if you look hard enough), you need to realize that what you are seeing isn't really the person but rather it's your reflection. You don't want to let this overwhelm you and turn it inward by saying, "What a terrible person I am because I see this." Rather, once you recognize a reflection of yourself, you can then decide to do something about it, or you can decide that it really isn't that important and that it doesn't matter. That way, you have learned how to progress positively to move on.

Suppose I'm a person who is ultra-fastidious about my clothing, and I would never wear anything with a tear. Then suppose I notice that you have a tear in your sweater. If I look upon that tear, the thought goes through my mind, "Gee, she is messy. She doesn't take care of her clothes." That is an incorrect perspective. What I am really seeing in that thought is a reflection of my own feeling toward how clothing should be cared for and worn. Maybe she tore her sweater on a nail while coming up the stairs. I must put this thought into the proper perspective. To do that, I must realize these two things: (1) This is an image of something inside of me; (2) It's an image that's not so important as to hold myself back in terms of awareness and growth. I go on from there. Keep it simple.

Consider that what you like about all the people in your life (pick those you have a great affection and affinity for) is what you like about you. They truly are your reflection. It's not what you want to be, it is what you really are. The reason that this is so important is that the depth of your feelings toward another individual is directly related to the depth of awareness in your own life. The more deeply aware you are of you, the more deeply aware you are of your reflection; in other words, of other people. In essence, as we go through life, none of us really matters to each other in the way that we have been brought up to think we do. We constantly try to lean on one another and to make outrageous demands. We say, "I exist because you are there, and you are helping me." In terms of reflection, none of that makes sense. What makes sense is that you are there, but I don't know who you are. I know who I am, and everything I know about you, I know about me. What you are to me is more of me telling me what I am.

What you then do is build an enormous foundation of self-awareness at greater and greater levels because you are in harmony with the Law of Reflection. As human beings, we pick people apart by saying, "She does this, and he does that." Every time you do that, you are taking pieces of yourself and throwing them away—a piece here and a piece there. You are dissipating yourself. It's like peeling off artichoke leaves until you are down to the heart, and even that isn't enough to satisfy you. You have thrown away a good portion of the plant instead of admitting that you don't know what another person is.

Everything you get in terms of reflection has something to tell you about yourself. You keep adding to yourself, and your stature gets larger and larger. This is why two people in love do so well. They increase their individual stature by seeing themselves in the reflection of the person they love. This is why, when you're in love, you feel larger, you feel bigger, you feel stronger, you feel taller, you feel like you can jump over the moon, or whatever. You have seen, at that one rare moment, the reality that what you are seeing is you and not them. Then, that picture dissipates because you immediately transfer the reflection of you to the other person and say, "What I love is him or her."

This is why I generally don't see a person as a person. I see a person as part of the reflection that I am involved in because I am reflecting upon myself. I am not really involved in the person. I am not busy making an identification of the individual along the way. Why should I be? Why should you? I am busy making an identification of me. When this is taken to its ultimate, you find that everyone you meet you already know because you know you. You are a stranger to no one. You can go anywhere in the world and meet people with any color skin, any philosophy, any religion, and you are perfectly at home with them. You know them because you know you, and they are simply a reflection of you. This is the ultimate unity of humanity.

It is not true that you seek out in another person a sense of acceptance or gratification or whatever word you want to use. You are really seeking yourself, and you are seeing if you can find yourself in another person. When you see your reflection, you are seeing a very small piece into an unlimited amount of variety and infinity. You have the bird's eye view through the keyhole of infinity. In many situations, you might be looking too hard for the wrong thing, never seeing what's there which ruins many relationships.

Everything within you is there. You may abhor violence, but there is a capacity for violence inside of you. You can dodge this by saying, "Well, I just came upon the incident." That has nothing to do with it. Every incident you come upon is part of your life, and it is a reflection of you. The simplest, the nicest, and the most horrible are all parts of your reflection. It does indicate that within you is that capacity, to whatever degree it may be. Whoever the participants, they are involved in an act of great karmic importance to them, and that's very important. You might say, "I see that they are making a mistake. By reflection, I can see that capacity within myself, karmically speaking." What reflects in you is that full range of emotional reaction you see in me. There is no such thing as living a life without past experience since you have had no beginning and no end. Therefore, there will always be something that you can connect to with knowledge to reflect upon. Everything shows you the unlimited variety that exists within you.

For example, if I am smiling, it's outward evidence of something that pleases me which is something that pleases you. If someone is angry at me and my smile is a sincere expression of the way I feel, the person will cease to be angry. The reason the person stays angry is that the smile is very often insincere. It is a façade of the way I feel, and the other person immediately picks up on the façade and does not react positively. For example, Roger is truly angry and points that anger at Karen. If Karen sees that Roger is really angry then Karen is reflecting the anger within herself back to Roger. However, if Karen does not truly see the anger in Roger and comes back with a counter reflection, as it were, by being honestly and truly warm and friendly, then Roger's anger will honestly dissipate. Roger will no longer be angry. This is one of the precepts in the New Testament of the Bible. It was Jesus' reaction of stability that turned around the whole situation of his protagonists. He refused to be anything other than the sincere person that he was, but the key word here is the <u>sincerity</u> of his being.

Let's take a single cell in your body as another example. You cannot observe the function of a single cell in your body. You don't know if that cell is pulsing or if it's moving or what it's doing. It may be in an organ, in a group of cells, or it may be the very fact that you can change your visual perception from this to that, which is part of your variety. Everything shows you the unlimited variety that exists within you. There is nothing too small for you to see the changes you can make.

There are no exceptions to these laws. The third Prime Law of Reflection applies to the relationship between you and a tree as much as it does to any other relationship you have. Relationships are basically a relationship to all of life. A tree is alive, and you see in the tree your life. The tree is growing, and you are growing. However, the tree does not operate with the same kind of consciousness in terms of analysis that you do. You have been given that unique reflection in consciousness. The tree's reflection is there, but it is on a different level of consciousness. It knows itself so perfectly that it never does see you. A tree does not know that a man is coming at it with an axe. Basically, all trees love you whether you are a man coming to hug it or a man coming to cut it down or a dog coming with another idea. In effect, the tree says, "I don't know because I only know myself." It has a pure status of *And God saw*. Trees are much purer than humans. At the present time and on all levels in the kingdom of nature, their degree of perception far exceeds ours as human beings. We should be far superior in perception, but we are not. They perceive themselves so well that they do not even have to perceive any reflection. People who deal with animals teach us this. This is what people love about animals. An animal is so perfectly couched in its own perception that it has an atmosphere that far exceeds relationships among human beings.

We do not have any idealistic levels of communication. In fact, we have very low, mundane levels of communication. Although, the Chinese people come closest with the thousands of characters combined in their language that can mean any number of things. The English language is very simplified which furthers the communication problem. How can we communicate accurately since none of us sees the same reflection? We all see ourselves in what we perceive. To some degree, it will always be slightly different. What something means to you is all that matters—so much so that you cannot even transfer what it means to you to someone else. You are only interested in what your perception is, regardless of what that is. Problems occur because another person will never see what you see until that person sees himself in your reflection of what you see. This is the problem in teaching and is the key point in the way I was taught. I don't want you to read the story and see what the story says. I want you to see what I see so that you can understand what I see, and you can take it from there and make your own reflection later on.

If you are to understand what you see, you must see what I see and then go on and see what you see. The whole art of teaching is that the student sees what the teacher sees and then progresses it to whatever he wants to see from that point on. If the student fails to see what the teacher sees, he is building his house on quicksand. Whatever he sees will never have a logical foundation to carry it forward to wherever he wants to go. The whole art of being a teacher is to be able to be aware of what the student needs to see. You must be aware of where he is, and then you must be aware of what he needs to see in order to see you. That is the communicative process; the student must see what the teacher sees in order to start the whole movement of reflection.

There is a difference in the meaning between "reflection" and "in reflection." In effect, we take all reflections from the surface reflection, not from the insides of an individual. Otherwise, you have a mixture of what they are, what you think they are, and what you are. You start making an analysis, and that is not using the Law of Reflection. As you become more and more aware of these reflections, you build up a greater and greater awareness at your point of reflection. You then realize as you go through life that you've seen so many reflections that everyone seems to be harmonious with you.

When you stand and look in a mirror, you really don't see all parts of yourself. Your eyes move quickly as you concentrate on your hair, your eyes, your tie, or your shirt. You discover the total picture by observing and separating parts of your reflection. Even when you stand back from a full-length mirror and look for the total impression, you don't have the total impression. You may think you do, but you don't. You've separated and reflected upon the parts that seem to be the most important to you at that time. We do the same thing with people. In reflection, we only see a part or a group of parts. What is important, in using the Law of Reflection, is that we integrate the reflection as a separate surface reflection that's come back to us. We realize that what we are seeing is a mirrored reflection of us. This can be pro or con, positive or negative, or whatever the case may be. Therefore, when you see another person, you are really not concerned with your relationship to that person. You are concerned with the reflection you are getting off of that person.

Over a period of years, reflections build themselves into your personal unity. Within the whole scope of what you know, everyone seems to fit in easily and naturally, and no one frightens you, confuses you, or stuns you anymore. You can appreciate all the variances of reflections. Can you see how we have developed the wrong precepts? There is really no way to hide from one another. We think we can, but we can't. Whatever your face shows me, I can find a reaction within myself. If I can't, then whatever you show me does not exist within me. What I am seeing is not what is true or untrue with you but what is true or untrue with me. That's what's important!

In spiritual universal terms, we are just not made to hide from one another because the Universe does not hide from Itself. All parts are known to all other parts. That's the whole idea of the Law of Reflection. The ultimate is that you become aware of the reflections from others and integrate those reflections as your reflections from within you. To you, all people become standards of reflections for you. After awhile, you become so integrated in a mass sense that, unless you deal with people who can share relatively stimulating conversations, you have nothing to talk about. You have passed through those basic levels through reflection, and you are not interested in conversing at those levels any longer.

This is progressive expansion. If everyone were to do that, conversations would be electric to say the least. However, this is not happening in the world, so we have repetition, which is very dangerous. Why? Because there's no repetition in the Universe. Nothing repeats itself exactly, and you are closely aligned to the Universe. Repetitive conversation doesn't bother the person who's not at the level of awareness to use the five Prime Laws of Manifestation for this planet, so the person just goes on and on in conversation, saying the same things over and over again. One of the first things you notice in your application of the laws is an enormous change in yourself. You seek out a higher level of response, almost like a thirsty man would seek out water, so you can go on and see another reflection. However, you don't have to go through the world rattling tin cans in order to do this. Let people go ahead and make their statements, and contribute accordingly as you go about trying to see a new reflection. Eventually, you will add a greater volume of reflections to yourself as you develop within the infinite laws.

The Story of Infinity is about the continuation of meeting and desiring a greater sense of reflection in concert with the Universe. You do this by interacting with yourself right where you are currently living. Basically, what this all comes down to is a growth factor. You might think that if everyone did this, the world would fall apart, and nobody would care. You know that's not true! Everyone would care more—not less—because there's a different empathy with everything and everyone when you are interacting with yourself. If what appears to be another's demise is your upset, then it is an upsetting personal condition within you.

And God saw that the light was good;

Genesis 1:4

Good, like many words in language, is what a mystic calls a non-word. It doesn't mean anything. How good is good? If you give a child a penny, that's good. If you give me a million dollars, that's good. It's a word that's relative to the situation and is not valid. There are a lot of words in language like this. They are there, and they mean absolutely nothing until they are explained in relationship to something else. The word *good* is used here to mean "acceptable." How good was it to God? Since the story deals with infinity, we are talking about Ultimate Good.

and God separated the light from the darkness.

Genesis 1:4

We understood that we could not have separation *in the very beginning* when we got to the business of *the heavens and the earth* because separation was not acceptable in universal terms. After reflection, the third Prime Law of Manifestation, we have, *and God separated the light from the darkness.* If we were to look at this literally, it would blow up everything that we've learned up to this particular point. We can't allow that, nor does the writer want to allow that to happen. This writer's code is omission. He tells you something impossible in order to tell you something that isn't there. He's not using numbers. He's using omission.

"Separation" doesn't mean separation. It means recognition. This is what we are doing right here. We are isolating words in order to recognize their meanings. We are separating one sentence from another and one word from another in order to recognize the variables, the facets, or the polarities of the condition. *And God separated the light from the darkness* is nothing more than an indication that, following the Law of Reflection, we now have the fourth Prime Law of Manifestation. What is it?

1. The first Prime Law of Manifestation for this planet is the Law of Sound.
2. The second Prime Law of Manifestation for this planet is the Law of Direction.

3. The third Prime Law of Manifestation for this planet is the Law of Reflection.
4. The fourth Prime Law of Manifestation for this planet is the Law of Recognition.

Even when we've gone through the phase of reflection, we are far from complete. What does it mean when you say, "I see you, but I don't see you. I see myself in you"? I don't know what it means when I say, "I see myself," because at this particular point I am just seeing a totality. In order for me to understand what I see that is in me, I must apply the Law of Recognition.

If I see something in you that is distasteful, which is at the negative end of the polarity (the receptive end of receiving the negativity), then I must find out the positive end of the polarity. In order for me to improve myself and be more aware, I cannot live in just one polarity. In other words, I must recognize what I see and, in effect, separate myself from what I see in order to be able to work on it, apply it, absorb it, or to use it in whatever way I wish.

This is part of the problem for a great number of people. In believing that they are correcting themselves or helping themselves, they make a blanket statement like this: "I see this is wrong with me." Then they turn around and say, "But I don't know what to do about it." The reason that they don't know what to do about it is they haven't followed the Law of Reflection. They don't recognize that they have to separate the positive from the negative, the good from the bad, the up from the down, or the left from the right. They have to hold up what they recognize (as we are doing here) word for word and statement by statement to examine it in order to see what it says, to see what its polarity might be, and to see what might be in-between the two polarities.

People don't do this. They say, "I really can't cope with this situation because the problem is too large, and I am just inundated by the whole thing." You must acknowledge the problem in <u>reflection</u>, but you cannot really see what you've acknowledged until you <u>separate</u> yourself for <u>recognition</u>. I say, "I can see myself in her when she's thinking because I'm thinking also." When I use the Law of Reflection, I can then say, "She's not thinking; I'm thinking." However, I must <u>recognize</u> to what degree and on what level that thought is true for me in order to understand what I am doing with the thought. I cannot simply walk away and say, "Well, I'm thinking." I know I'm thinking, but what am I thinking about? I might be thinking about the horse races or about doing any number of things other than what I'm really dealing with at the moment. This is why it's sometimes hard to really understand what an author is telling you when you read a book. He or she is not speaking to you. Therefore, you are not operating on sound, the first Prime Law of Manifestation. No matter how profound the writing is, you find your mind wandering because you don't have a good reflection from the author to you. When you don't have a good reflection, you don't have a valid recognition of ideas. The book doesn't become pertinent to your whole being until you start talking about it.

When you are reading a book, you can say out loud that you don't know if you believe what you are reading or not. You can actually carry on a verbal conversation with yourself. In doing that, you are <u>reflecting</u> upon what you are reading, and you begin to <u>recognize</u> what the author is trying to tell you. You are using the third and fourth Prime Laws of Manifestation, which are the Law of Reflection and the Law of Recognition, respectively. This is why we have the truism that, in teaching your students, you shall be taught. They allow you to use the Law of Sound so that eventually the ideas can be <u>reflected</u> upon, <u>recognized</u>, and understood. That makes you smart, but of course, this depends on how sincere you are about using the laws.

There is a particular need on earth for you to fulfill the third and fourth laws. Let's put this in terms of the planet itself. We have talked about reflecting off of individuals and separating and recognizing, but this is also true of your experiences, in other words, the events. How do you know when an event begins, and where the line of will starts or leaves off? You must see yourself in the reflection of the experience. At that point, you must be able to recognize (separate) whether you are seeing the event or whether you are seeing a continuation of the will. In order to do this, you must separate yourself from the event. We have already determined that *darkness* means receptivity and *light* means activity. The Law of Recognition reminds us that active and receptive energies are polarities of one another: *and God separated the light from the darkness.*

And God called the light Day and the darkness he called Night.

Genesis 1:5

Your ears need to perk up. The word *said* has already been used, so why did the writer introduce the new word *called*? The activity of energy is infinite, but on a manifested planet it's going to be unusable if it stays infinite. It has to reach a finite point to go on to the next cycle of infinity. Therefore, in order to turn light into finitude, light is named. It is *called Day*. Light and darkness have already been established in universal polarity, and now they are going to be defined.

Can day be night and night be day? Of course they can't. One exists in the absence of the other. The universal concept of light and darkness still applies. What must be done here is to take the universal terms of *light* and *darkness* and make them finite. They've been separated to the point of finite awareness. *Light* and *darkness* have now been defined and named *Day* and *Night*. *And God called the light Day and the darkness he called Night.* That is as finite as *light* and *darkness* could possibly become. Finite awareness, then, is the fifth Prime Law of Manifestation. Awareness is part of the law because we must be aware of when day is day and night is night. In other words, we cannot intermingle the meaning of the two polarities. In the construction and the organization of the planet and its orbit around the sun, there is a constant condition wherein half of the planet is in day and half of the planet is in night. Half of the world in day, and half of the world in night are definitive of the Law of Finite Awareness.

In using the fifth Prime Law of Manifestation, the Law Finite Awareness, you are meant to be aware of the finitude. I see in you only me (the Law of Reflection). I recognize what it is that I see in me (the Law of Recognition), so I am now finitely aware of the finite totality. The Law of Finite Awareness is clear, crisp, and clean with no fuzzy edges, and that's how I am going to use it. Day is day and night is night. I see day clearly as an active position, and I see night clearly as a receptive position; I do not and cannot mix the two. This is a very high degree of depth to full awareness as it pertains to polarities.

And there was evening and there was morning, the first day.

Genesis 1:5

Initially we had, *And God called the light Day and the darkness he called Night.* When *darkness* and *light* went to *Night* and *Day*, we were getting down to a finite position. Now we have *morning*, and we have *evening*, where the mystical writer keys us into manifestation by saying, *And there was evening and there was morning, the first day*. This is the finite awareness of the final definition for action. This is very important because we know the mystical writer will not repeat anything for repetition's sake. He repeats in order to provide an expansion, as it were, and to provide us with tools to use.

Within the first four Prime Laws of Manifestation, nothing was established on the tri-level condition of this planet. We went from darkness to light and from night to day, but now we go from evening to morning. We have three separate definitions at three distinct levels to consider and use. We are being given the totality, with this very first view of the spiritual, mental, and physical levels. When you recognize yourself on these three levels, you become self-aware. All that you are aware of at those moments of self-awareness is an instantaneous burst of intelligence in thought. If we were able to freeze the action at those moments, all we would see, in its true form, is your all-consuming awareness of energy. What we really do, in terms of self-recognition and self-awareness, is to do exactly that. We stop action, and at any one of those given moments, we can know ourselves in totality.

You might ask, "If we have point A here and point B there, don't these points begin to build up in which we are aware of the totality?" Yes, we are aware of the totality, but we are no longer aware of the building blocks (the details) that got us to that point in our awareness. They have become part of the total mass of our being. We feel a greater sense of being without feeling greatness in any one of those parts of our being. For instance, I don't feel that I am more intelligent now than I was ten years ago. All I know is that I am a more aware person and in the contribution of all things, intelligence plays a part. If I were to identify, in my mind, how much of a part intelligence plays, I wouldn't know. I can't tell you, nor would you know. I might be a nicer person now than I was ten years ago, but I don't know what has made me nicer. Or, I might be worse for that matter, but I don't know what has brought me to this point. I can go around and say, "I'm really a nice guy," but you can say something that irritates me, and in that moment (whether I thought I was a nice guy or not), I'm still going to show the reflection of antagonism because that's what I am at that moment. I'm only aware of the totality as the moment sees itself in reflection.

Suppose that you and I couldn't get along. In all human endeavors, it was just not workable. With that being a fact, we would both be foolish to pursue a course of interaction. It would be wise to recognize (separate) and not see each other. I go on in my terms of awareness and reflect off of other people, many of whom will begin to show me that which was in me that reflected off of you. I start building on those reflections momentarily and on a totally aware basis. Years later, you and I come back together, and we seem to get along reasonably well. We can communicate. We have not changed toward each other at all. Only I have changed and only you have changed within ourselves. Each of us changed because we built a totality on our own awareness by moving ourselves away from a block that previously did not seem workable to either one of us.

You will find this to be a truism in every serious argument you have ever had with another person, whether male or female. When you accuse someone of something that they almost vehemently deny, you are really telling them what it is that you see in yourself. You are probably arguing with yourself about how you would do what they seem to be doing because of your reflection off of the situation. That is why they argue with you and deny your accusations. You just cannot know another person! Such situations should actually be easier because everything is predicated upon your ability to know your own awareness at which time you are doing what the Universe does. You become totally aware of yourself. You don't have to increase your awareness of a specific situation or another person because you are always seeing yourself. What you do is increase your positive self-awareness. Period.

A mystical writer doesn't write in any way but progression. He never writes anything out of context. Everything follows everything else in the way it is supposed to follow. You must understand that nothing is thrown in just because the story is there. If you're at a point of reflection and having a great deal of difficulty from the reflection, and you know that you are having a great deal of difficulty from the reflection, then you are not getting to that point of awareness. At such a time, it is wise for you to consider that you have abdicated (or you have somehow missed in some shape or form) steps one and two, the first two Prime Laws of Manifestation — the Law of Sound and the Law of Direction, in that order.

You might ask, "How can I miss the Law of Sound?" That's very easy. Many black thoughts pass through your mind when you are upset. Did you ever stop and speak those thoughts out loud to yourself? If so, did you not realize that what you were saying was almost an insult to your own "beingness"? That is the use of the Law of Sound. Many times, you might have to say to that thought in your mind, "I have a black thought, and I am really upset with him." You then say out loud for yourself to hear, "I am really fed up with him." Then you say to yourself, "That's a stupid thing for me to say. I'm acting like a child when I say that." Your next step is to use the Law of Direction and say to yourself, "Look, forget this. It's ridiculous to act this way, and it isn't doing me any good. I am lowering my own standard by thinking and acting this way." Now, you have taken into consideration the second Prime Law of Manifestation, the Law of Direction.

When you meet up with him at a later time, you are then free to use the Law of Reflection because you can see in him your ability to deal with yourself. This carries you on to the Law of Recognition, but it's possible that you might have to go to the first Law of Sound many times while you are learning. I don't think that the average person (even though there is no such animal) ever uses the Law of Sound. That means that when he is upset, which amounts to a block in his whole growth awareness, he keeps turning his thoughts around and around in his head. That way, he never uses the Law of Sound. He can't start the ball rolling and use the other laws, and he ends up bitter and frustrated. It's difficult, then, for him to get along with himself or with other people.

When we don't use the Law of Sound inside our own room, inside our own car, or inside our own shower, we take our troubles to other people. We are using them in order to use the Law of Sound, and we call those people "friends." We unload on them. We are actually going to a particular point, using the Law of Sound, and re-directing the energy. Unfortunately when we do that, we don't have the awareness that we should have because we are asking others to give us the Law of Direction: "Please give me my direction because here is my problem." But, this is not what should be happening. You are meant to be working out your own direction by reflecting on what the next step is that you need to take. Then, you separate yourself from the situation in order to recognize where it is that you want to go or what you want to do, and you go on from there. This sequence is all part and parcel of our lives, but we are not using these universal laws in their correct form and sequence.

If God had only <u>thought</u> that this planet should come into being and never <u>did</u> anything more than go to the third Law of Reflection, none of this planet could have existed. What you want to arrive at, as a totally aware being, is simply that you cannot exist if you do not take the first Law of Sound and run through this sequence properly because you cannot start these laws somewhere in the middle. You can't say, "Let's start with the Law of Reflection." You know this doesn't mean that you have to go through this sequence <u>every</u> time you meet someone or <u>every</u> time you are in any situation. This is why the word *and* appears so many times in the story. What you have in these laws is a continuation of a whole program for living. It helps to know what's going on!

You are actively receiving, but you are actively acting upon that which you are receiving. You are in a receptive state primarily and in an active state secondarily. Your ability to separate anything from anything increases. You'll find that you will sleep when you wish to sleep because you set up your own day and night principle. In terms of finite awareness, you know where you are. All of your activities are based on going through these five Prime Laws and living within them. You then know what's going on, almost as a fleeting recognition but with full awareness.

This is never a static position. Here you are at point A, but you are going on to point B. You know that you're at point A moving to point B, and you're very much aware of yourself as you pass through point A to point B, to point C, to point D, and to every other point as you keep going. The problem lies when you are first trying to apply the laws. You are very much like the little child who is learning how to run. Your coordination is very awkward, but you follow along and you say to yourself, "Wait a minute. The harmony of the planet is in the laws of Sound, Direction, Reflection, Recognition, and Finite Awareness." After awhile, this becomes very natural for you as part of your consciousness fully grown to itself. At that point, you use the laws without feeling any kind of static stops along the way. However, occasionally you might need to pause, which is perfectly alright. It's possible that you want a greater finite awareness at certain points, so you do an evaluation to see if you've skipped over something.

When you finish your experience here and make your transition to go on, there is a reckoning that takes place, and you run up your own balance sheet. No one else does this for you. It is a disastrous thing at that particular juncture of your experience to look back and recognize that you have not done a damn thing for yourself. In terms of your own personal progress, you haven't <u>gone</u> anywhere. When you work out your ledger sheet, which is the karma assigned to you as part of your growth experience, you realize that you didn't accomplish anything.

Your responsibility is to be the best conceivable person that you can be. Your responsibility to the children is to show them the most proper, most honorable, and the most spiritual way of living as you know it to be. You set the example, and they choose whether they wish to follow it or not. That is the extent of your responsibility to them. You have got to teach the children, but you teach them on the assumption that you know what you are doing, leaving them to make the determination of whether they want to follow those precepts or not.

I teach you in terms of what I know, and here it is. If you can use the knowledge, that's fine. However, it is up to you if you want to use it or not. I don't call you up and say, "How are you doing? Are you using the teachings correctly? Give me a report, and you are grounded for a week because you didn't do this right." It's not my responsibility to do that, nor is it any parent's responsibility to do that either.

Dissatisfaction comes from the realization that you are not functioning in harmony with these laws. But remember, you are always going to disturb some people. Those who are not using the Law of Reflection are afraid to see that you're moving on because you've reached a point in your awareness that has been integrated and is now a part of you. You are ready to move on, and if there's anything that people dislike, it's to see somebody ready to speed away.

One of the things that we don't have built into us is the ability to judge anything other than ourselves. Now this is a really important statement because it leads into a lot of areas that I am very, very definite about, and I think you will eventually become definite about them also. You do not have any mechanism to judge anything or anyone but yourself. Judgment of yourself is in the laws of Reflection, Recognition and then Finite Awareness. If we have twelve men in a jury box who say, "tried and guilty," then we have twelve men in a jury box who are guilty. If they see the guilt in another person, they see the guilt in themselves. This refers back to the New Testament where Jesus says, *He who is among you without sin, let him first throw a stone at her.* (John 8:7). This simply means that if we can see guilt in someone else, we can see the guilt in ourselves. Since we cannot judge, we cannot presume. It is the Law of Reflection. You don't know how an event is going to turn out, and neither do I. I have a great deal of ability to prognosticate, but even then, I wouldn't presume and you can't presume either. You have to go according to only one thing, and that is to ask yourself, "Is this important for me?" You cannot justly say if someone else is benefiting or not. They may be putting on a façade that appears to be anything other than what they're really thinking, feeling, and doing.

How could you ever presume an outcome from using these laws since we cannot presume anything in reflection? Nowhere in these laws is there any indication of presumption of any kind. You might say that it appears that there's irritation between you and someone else that's causing irritation, but you really don't know that to be true. You're seeing a façade that appears to give you an impression. You may be having a profound effect upon that individual as a result of his reflection on the situation. You know you're having a profound effect upon yourself. Therefore, presumption of how these effects are going to work out is beyond your capability and comprehension, and it's a violation of the basic workings of the law.

I recognize that some of you may resist this idea, but I am only quoting to you what I know to be true. The Universe does not have any gray areas. It is black, and it is white. There are laws here, and the laws do not have any fringe areas in them. You either do it A, or you do it B, but you can't do A½ plus and B½ minus. The laws are very cut and dried. You may ask how this can be since that doesn't allow for any changes, any interaction, or any ability to get along. The laws themselves are so perfectly formed that you don't need fringe areas. According to the laws, everything is right. The law is the law is the law. The closer to the laws, the more perfect the action.

You might say that all of this is too hard to go along with. But, don't you understand that every lifeline is different for every individual because it's peculiar to each individual on the basis of his or her own karmic assignment? Here's how it works: I have one lifeline. As I deal with each one of you, you are giving me a reflection. What each of you is showing me is that my lifeline is infinite, plus or minus. You allow me to learn the infinite expansion of my lifeline wherever I can find myself at anytime. I'll never run out of possibilities while walking on my lifeline of the law in terms of harmony. Remember, it's <u>your</u> experience with yourself not someone else's experience. When you recognize something, you are ready to deal with it. You have got to have something coming back to you for you to reflect upon. Otherwise, you will never recognize it because you cannot see a reflection of an image that you cannot see is there. This is such a stringent requirement for some mystics that they stay up on the mountaintop and will never come down. They do not want anything to interfere with their lifeline in terms of their adherence to the exact letter of the law.

At this point in the Story of Infinity, there are no more Prime Laws of Manifestation. We have come to the first numerical movement in the story. The fact that the writer has now used a number, *the first day*, indicates the end of the five Prime Laws. Everything else in this story pertains directly to what has now manifested on Planet Earth. We are now going to deal with the first esoteric meaning of a number: the number 1.

And there was evening and there was morning, the first day. What is the esoteric meaning of the number 1 in terms of how this planet is going to operate? How are we designed to live harmoniously with the laws created for this planet? It's not enough to say that *the first day* was the beginning. What comes before the first number—the first day? Before we start anything in our lives, it behooves us to recall the exact sequence of creation given to us in these five Prime Laws of Manifestation: Sound, Direction, Reflection, Recognition, and Finite Awareness.

In just these first five verses of the Story of Infinity, we are given the exact rules about how to start anything. We use sound to direct and reflection to recognize for finite awareness. Then and only then are we prepared to begin anything. Most failures basically occur because people have not prepared themselves to begin by using these five Prime Laws of Manifestation for this planet. However, Planet Earth demands that we use these Prime Laws before we take initial movements to start anything. If we don't, it's like saying we're going to issue forth a baby—and zing! Here comes the baby! We haven't allowed time for the tissues, bones, nervous system, brain, and other organs to form. It's as if we just hoped everything would turn out okay, and that's not possible. It takes time for the preparation to occur. However, isn't that the way we often operate our lives? We just start and hope. We fail to recognize that in the laws of creation for this planet, there is a necessary sequence before beginning, before the first number. It takes time to prepare.

What we have here are some of the most vital and enormous tools to get anything underway. If we were to stop right here and right now, we could go through our lives never making an error. Now, we are prepared to begin.

Discussion Questions

Can anyone or anything stop the natural progression of energy?

What is the planet's first initial activity following sound?

How does the Law of Direction operate in your experience?

In what ways do you increase your self-awareness by using the Law of Reflection?

Why doesn't the word *good* mean anything?

What does the Law of Recognition mean to you?

In what ways does the Law of Finite Awareness indicate infinite possibilities?

Why don't you have the ability to judge anyone other than yourself?

Why is it necessary to follow the five Prime Laws of Manifestation in sequential order?

What comes before beginning?

THREE

The Basic Elements of Creation

And there was morning and there was evening, the first day.

Genesis 1:5

In the continuation of this whole program for living, we must be aware about what's going on. What happens if you accept something that isn't satisfactory to you as you go through the stages in the five Prime Laws of Manifestation? What happens is that you don't begin! This occurs most frequently with people who ignore the last three laws: the Law of Reflection, the Law of Recognition, and the Law of Finite Awareness. They stop the process after the Laws of Sound and Direction. It's also possible that in following these precepts you need to change your degree of receptivity. Maybe you skipped over something, and you need to do a more thorough evaluation. In that case, drop whatever it is you're doing because you don't have the basic requirements in place to start. Your lifeline has peculiarities based on what you need, but you still need to prepare within the great blueprint provided for this planet in the five Prime Laws.

Sometimes, this is nothing more than saying you will or will not do something and then following the characteristics that best suit you, based on what you intend to accomplish. Often, you can do this and still stay within the confines of these laws. In relationships, individuals often realize that something is wrong from the very beginning. Their beginning is built on marshmallows. They just grit their teeth and keep going along blindly with absolutely nothing to support the natural function of harmony within the laws. The key to success hinges on the first step. With the momentum of the Universe behind you, it's like sailing with your back to the wind. This is no different than looking at the engine of a car in which one spark plug is placed incorrectly. Even if all other parts of the engine are absolutely perfect that one spark plug can be enough to make the whole engine malfunction. You wouldn't overhaul the whole engine just because one spark plug is out of place. That would be a waste of time and money. You pull out the spark plug, put it back in properly, and the engine functions once again. We are all spark plugs. If we go around trying to overhaul the damn engine, we don't set ourselves up to spark properly. What this amounts to is that the whole operative function is taken care of by universal law. All you have to do is your particular part at your particular point. Can you live with the alternative?

It's extremely important to understand that the elements which bring about the beginning of anything cannot be done for you. You cannot go to someone and ask for that kind of help because another person cannot give you <u>your</u> reflection. Other people can only give you their reflection. No one knows how you are going to see something because your reflection is very personal to you.

There are no more <u>Prime</u> Laws of Manifestation. The fact that the mystical writer has used a number, *the first day*, indicates the first numerical movement and the end of the five Prime Laws. Everything else, from this point on in the story, pertains directly to this planet that has now been manifested. The writer didn't put *the first day* on the very first line of the story because there is no beginning in infinity. We needed the five Prime Laws of Manifestation to come before the number 1. Now, we have to consider the esoteric meaning of 1 in terms of how it's going to operate as the basic numerological value for this particular place in space. It's not enough to say that *the first day* is the beginning. Behind the beginning (1) is the exact sequence of how we must begin anything and everything in our lives: Sound, Direction, Reflection, Recognition (separation), and Finite Awareness — in that order.

THE BASIC ELEMENTS OF CREATION

And God said, Let there be a firmament in the midst of the waters, and let it divide the waters from the waters.

Genesis 1:6

In just one sentence, *waters* is mentioned three times. Remember, the esoteric writer is not going to waste anything in repetition. Every word is vitally important to the whole meaning. Although he has mentioned *waters* here three times, he is not referring literally to water. Earlier, we learned that water symbolically represents spirituality, so what is the firmament dividing? The firmament divides spiritual-spiritual, spiritual-mental, and spiritual-physical. These are the three levels of construction on this plane for this planet. The writer has set up an attitude for every level of consciousness, which is a tripod for our planet, and this is done in spiritual terms first. Why can we make such a statement? To begin with, the planet's initial reflection was the spirit (the essence) of God reflecting upon the waters. The place had already been prepared with initial characteristics couched in spiritual terms, and we know there isn't any break in the story because the writer continues to indicate continuity with the use of the word *and*.

Let there be a firmament in the midst of the waters [1], *and let it divide the waters* [2] *from the waters* [3]. Here are the three levels of the spiritual, mental, and physical for the very "beingness" of this planet. Remember, humanity has not arrived yet. The writer isn't talking about you and me yet. He is talking about the three basic levels of the planet that are couched in these three terms: spiritual-spiritual, spiritual-mental, and spiritual-physical. More than ever, this substantiates how we are to act and how we are to deal with each other because everything on the planet is couched in spiritual terms.

And God made the firmament, and divided the waters that were under the firmament from the waters that were above the firmament; and it was so.

Genesis 1:7

In terms of *firmament*, we are talking about energy. A firmament, as you can perhaps see in the sky, is a vortical energy force. What was once an original, single vortex is split apart and becomes a separate vortex. The firmament is dividing the energy not the waters.

And God called the firmament Sky. And there was evening and there was morning, the second day.

Genesis 1:8

The earth and the sky do not have the same vortex. These are two different vortical movements. By splitting the initial vortex and dividing it into two, the vortical energy has changed. We can look up into the sky, but we cannot see the air. Yet, when we look down at the ground, we see the ground. The energy frequency of the ground is slower than the energy frequency of the air. Initially, they were all one but then the firmament (the vortex) split the slower frequency from the faster frequency. We do the same thing all the time. We take an atom and send an energy stream into the atom, thereby splitting the atom apart and causing two more forces to exist. If we do this under controlled conditions, we can basically construct anything we want as a result of splitting the energy. The more we learn, the more we find out that we can send one energy vortex to split another energy vortex. We can do any number of things as a result of energy fusion, and when that science fully matures, we'll eventually have full control over most of the energy on this planet. Nature does this in terms of crystals. A crystal splits light waves that are basically white, and the light waves cause rainbow spectrums. Energy fusion occurs all the time right in front of our eyes.

Up to now in the story, we have considered that *let there be* indicates direction. It showed us that we were at a point of readiness to *let* it happen. Also, the constant use of the word *and* shows us that the writer has done nothing to interrupt the continuity for the next movement to logically occur. Nothing new has been introduced. Once the spiritual, mental, and physical elements have been established, it's time to have order.

And God called the firmament Sky. Nothing is mentioned about earth. Only *Sky* has been named as the upper firmament. *And there was evening and there was morning, the second day.* How is it possible to have two, *the evening* and *the morning*, in these terms when we have only one *Sky*?

Evening and *morning* have already been defined, and the writer isn't going to do that twice. Therefore, we don't have an opposite polarity yet. Only one is named in order for us to understand that if we separate one, what do we have? We have the Law of Separation, which is two. How can I separate 1 of anything without having 2 of something? 2 proves 1. In the Story of Infinity, the writer is telling you that the esoteric meaning of the number 2 is "to separate." The application of the number 2, as we are meant to deal with it, is to balance or to see what the separation has left us. The two parts may not be equal, but that's not the point. We are trying to see what's left from the process of separation.

We know that the esoteric meaning of the number 1 is *beginning*, but is *beginning* the right word for the number 1? No, because if I say to you that the number 1 means *beginning*, you can turn around and ask what *beginning* means. What does *beginning* mean? It means that you can begin by applying sound, direction, reflection, recognition (or separation), and finite awareness. Now you have a full explanation of what *beginning* means.

If I say that the number 2 means "balance," you don't know what "balance" means until you take something and separate it. When you separate it, depending upon the weight of either piece, you can understand balance. I can only give you 2 after I have separated 1 because 2 is the next sequence, and the sequence of the numbers is very important. The application of the number 2 is to first separate from 1 and then weigh and balance the results. The writer is telling us, literally and mathematically, how the planet is going to operate.

I'm sure you've heard it said that the conclusion of anything is at the beginning. Such a statement is our non-time factor. There is no past, there is no future, there is only now. There is only now because the beginning, which has not yet been divided, is the totality of the whole. It is your beginning, your middle, and your end. Therefore, if you produce the proper beginning, you are assured of the proper ending, and if you do not produce the proper beginning, you are assured of an improper ending. This is why the beginning of anything is so vitally important.

The beginning runs through its normal growth before transitioning to the next logical step, which is to separate itself. Here's an example: Assume that you've been accepted by a college. Your next step would be to leave home. As a rule, you leave in order to separate that life from your college life. Your life has been split into two: one off-campus life and one on-campus life. The reason that we don't see experiences so clearly is that we do so much on a daily basis that we're constantly producing beginnings and separations. We're not as aware of what's happening as we should be. When we come into contact with others, in terms of relationships, we should be aware right away. That's why lovers experience such terrible pain when they separate from one another. Together, they feel like one, which is always a beginning. When they are apart, there is the separation from that unity.

The writer was very, very wise. If he had said, "There is the sky, and there is the earth," he would have violated the whole meaning. That would have already told you that the esoteric meaning of the number 2 was "balance." It's not "balance" because you cannot have balance until you weigh something that has been separated to make the two. Do you see how intelligently it was done? Look at the tremendous esoteric thought that goes into that statement. By omission, you have to realize exactly what was meant. By establishing the division in the sky, the writer now gives you everything you need to know, but you have to take a few steps beyond that.

THE BASIC ELEMENTS OF CREATION 57

And God said, Let the waters that are under the sky be gathered together in one place, and let the dry land appear; and it was so.

Genesis 1:9

The writer is establishing the separation, and he could go on forever separating *the waters* from *the dry land* because he's already established the fourth Prime Law of Manifestation: the Law of Recognition (separation). In this particular case, he's now beginning to tell you how the planet was being formed and how it's going to be used in terms of its laws and its existence.

From the separation of 1, we get 2, but the two parts are not necessarily equal in size or balanced. All division amounts to the same thing: 1 is always separated to give us 2 of something. Then, 2 of something can be adjudged for what it is, or we can divide it again and find something else. This is the basis of mathematics as well as the whole system of the Universe, as far as we're concerned, because the Universe is constantly dividing Itself. It takes Its unity, which It will never lose, and constantly divides that unity into parts. The parts divide themselves into parts, but they never leave the unity. The Universe can divide Itself infinitely and still be the Universe because It started by dividing the only thing It is to begin with. All divisions remain part of the unity.

We can recognize this division by all the many people in the world. Each person is a division within the Universe. I am universal. You are universal. Each of us is a divided piece of the universal whole. The male sperm and the female egg aren't really separate entities. Both have parts of the other, but each has a dominance of one. In a sperm, there exists the male and female (the plus and minus polarities) even though the masculine is dominant. The same is true for the female egg, where the feminine is dominant. By coming together, they produce a third unit. In essence, they were divided on one hand and are united on the other, only to divide again. When they join together, they unitize the whole as another unit and still with the division of male and female within; although, one is perhaps more dominant.

A cell is dividing life, in the continuation of life, as it expresses in different forms. To carry this concept even further, everyone is really two-sided. We are literally divided right down the middle. If you physically examine yourself carefully, you will see this to be true. Your left side is not the same as your right side, and you can see that division exists even within your own unity.

The Universe isn't splitting apart from Itself. It's still the Universe with Its own character, which allows any part of Itself to join again and to become part of Its original character. You always have the ultimate potential of being universal because you've never been divided or taken away from the Original Source. You are the Original Source. Understanding this, you can do two things with your life as an interesting adventure. You can try to identify yourself as that divided part and see the Universe within you, or you can try to refuse identifying yourself as divided and see yourself and the Universe back in unity. You have this choice at any given time.

The mystic who likes being a mystic in the ultimate sense of the word practices forgetting that he has been divided and spends his whole life trying to recapture his basic unity on a universal level. I think you and I would prefer to identify our part, identify the Universe in that part, and then go ahead and use it from there, knowing that at any point we can always go to the universal oneness because we never left it. If you take a bucket, put it in the ocean, and never pull it out, there's a certain amount of water in the bucket. While it's divided from the rest of the ocean by a thin wall, it's still the ocean water. You see the water in the bucket as ocean water, and it is. If you take it out of the ocean, it is still ocean water—slightly separated but with all the qualities of the ocean. If you pour the water back into the ocean, you can't identify it. It's the same thing. The walls of the bucket appear to be a logical barrier between water here and water there. Even if you boil it and it becomes vapor, it's still ocean water vapor that eventually becomes clouds, which become rain which eventually goes back into the ocean. The properties always remain, even during the changes. If you were to boil the water on the stove and see the steam rise, you would say that's just steam. That may be true, but that's steam from the ocean water, and given enough time, it will eventually go back to its original source.

Once the Law of Recognition (separation) existed, the process of separation could be used in the formation of the planet. Obviously, there had to be form to receive you and me and all mankind in terms of consciousness.

And God called the dry land Earth; and the gathering together of the waters he called Seas; and God saw that it was good.

Genesis 1:10

The mystical writer continues to show us separation. *And there was evening and there was morning, the second day* shows the Law of Recognition (separation) that gives us our <u>ability</u> to separate. This is our spiritual separation. *Let the waters that are under the sky be gathered together in one place, and let the dry land appear* is the <u>application</u> of the law, which is our mental separation. *And God called the dry land Earth; and the gathering together of the waters he called Seas* is the <u>physical separation</u>.

The writer repeats these things emphatically because he wants you to understand the importance. Here, he is telling you that, in division, you must also recognize the three levels of existence. You cannot just divide on the physical level and the physical level only. He is telling you that, in order to determine balance, harmony, or anything you want to determine from the two pieces, you must determine the separation on all three levels before you have an honest determination. The mystical writer insists you must understand these three levels in order to understand that the Universe is constantly separating and dividing Itself, but It is still the Universe.

Any separation cannot be held at one distinct level and be kept away from its other two levels. That's the reality of separation. Always consider separation from the one, and therefore complete to the one, at any given time. Men and women appear to operate as separate beings, but that isn't really a separation. Females have a spiritual being and so do males. Females have a mental being and a physical being and so do males. Yet, we look at each other and believe that we are separated and that we are different because females have this construction and males have that construction. The writer is telling you that you cannot do that in separation. Males must look at females and females have to look at males and recognize that they are meant to find, within that separation, the basic one unity. Neither one of them ever leaves the unity of the Universe. You and I have never left one another.

Separation has a great deal to do with the wonderful Law of Reflection. I don't see you. I see me. When I see me, I can see a separation by identification. Then, I immediately realize that, as long as I am seeing separation, I must consider it from each of the spiritual, mental, and physical levels. The minute I do that, I not only see me, but I see you and I see the whole Universe. Now, we are on universal terms again. You and I are talking on those higher levels.

Therefore, what I see in me is more than you. It encompasses me, you, him, her, them, and as much as I want it to encompass relative to my degree of universal understanding. The mystic writes this way so that you don't get confused and miss the meaning.

This is very peculiar to the outworking of the laws of number 1 and number 2. We have the five Prime Laws that precede the beginning for 1 and are brought into separation and balance for the number 2. The Prime Laws magnify and brings us the beginning. Right at this particular point, the writer wants you to understand that all things are tri-level. All things are rotated, inverted, turned, and worked within themselves, no matter what you think you've done. He is establishing, more than anything else, the premise that you cannot separate yourself from the Universe. Period. You just cannot separate yourself, and nothing else can either. You cannot hold up something and say this is different from the source from which you have drawn it, just like the water in the bucket drawn from the ocean water is still ocean water.

And God said, Let the earth bring forth vegetation, the herb yielding seed after its kind, and the fruit tree yielding fruit after its kind, wherein is their seed, upon the earth; and it was so.

Genesis 1:11

We have finished the second day, but we are not into the third day at this point in the story. We know that the writer is giving us continual direction with *And God said, Let . . .* The law is going to happen, and it's going to follow this particular precept. He has given us something here so earthshaking that we cannot possibly gloss over it. Also, writers change right here. The new mystical writer has gone from the separation principle into basic laws of life on Planet Earth. We must not miss this enormous change from the technicality of separation to the Law of Survival and the Law of Growth. The word *vegetation* has just popped up in the story, and he tells us what *vegetation* is: *the herb yielding seed after its kind, and the fruit tree yielding fruit after its kind, wherein is their seed, upon the earth; and it was so.*

What is the law? It is the Law of Karma. Like produces like. Pound this into your head so that every time you stand in front of a mirror, you reflect upon it. Everything produces exactly and only after its own kind. You cannot have a result or an effect that does not exactly parallel its initial cause. The philosophy that says you are born, you die, and then you come back as a butterfly is so unreasonably unreasonable that to give it any credence for more than two-tenths of a second magnifies ignorance. Man produces man. He may produce low-level man, but he is producing man. Corn produces corn, not flowers and not roses. Seeds produce seeds, trees produce trees, and this is all that can be produced.

The first basic law of life established on the planet is that cause produces an exact effect. This is so very important to us. So far, we've gone through very intricate and basic knowledge in this Story of Infinity. The Law of Recognition (separation) has now broken off to give us the first basic law of life. Man has still not yet arrived. These planetary laws were set in before humans arrived, and these laws will affect everything that's here and everything that will follow. This also means that every thought equals itself in every thought or its action. You cannot think ill of someone but do good and think that the doing good changes the ill thought. Ill produces ill, and good produces good. Whatever the case may be, like produces like. This is an exact law. We are back to the black and white. The law is not variable.

You cannot say that you partially understood. You either understood, or you didn't. If you understood, then you understood to a degree and that's all you understood. The result is how far you are going to go with this degree of understanding. We go through life and say, "That's what I said, but that's not what I meant." Or, "I did that, but that's not what I meant to do." You simply cannot live your life that way because that's a major violation of the earth's operation. If you live this life in a spiritually exemplary manner, then the next one will follow accordingly and equal to that particular form of endeavor. You can't buy your way into heaven. You can't leave your estate to establish a school of theology and say that this is going to make up for being a rat all your life. It just doesn't work that way.

Man may have walked on all fours at one time on this planet, but he has always been a thinking man with consciousness. He was never anything but a human being. He has always been able to make his determinations and his analyses with his own ability to live within the law. He may have looked very crude at one time, but he was still a man. Butterflies, horses, dogs, and cats belong to the nature pool of energy. The energy that activates the butterfly is the same energy that's brought back into nature and used again in the natural kingdom. Next time, the nature pool of energy can be used to birth a horse or a dog or another butterfly because the energy is always an animal energy just as your energy, in terms of human consciousness, is always human consciousness.

The mystical writer says, "Like produces like." He doesn't say, "Like attracts like." Go to the writer's words: *the herb yielding seed <u>after its kind</u>, and the fruit tree yielding fruit <u>after its kind</u>*. Are we sure that like attracts like? We're sure that like <u>produces</u> like, but are we sure that like attracts like? The Law of Polarity and the Law of Cause and Effect are both valid, but the writer is talking about the Law of Cause and the Effect here. "Like attracts like" is the Law of Polarity. The interesting thing is that either one of these laws carried out to some infinite line will produce the other law.

If I take the Law of Polarity (two opposites) and carry it out far enough, I will find that the opposites start producing each other and that they are no longer opposites. But if I take the Law of Cause and Effect (karma) and carry it out far enough, I will find that somewhere along the line, it will produce opposites. This gives us a graph that is very interesting. If I take any linear line and extend it into infinity, it will eventually develop into a circle. Since one of these laws extended far enough will start producing the other and vice-versa, what really happens in infinity is that the linear line will start to curve and then will start to curve again. The line starts to twist and becomes the sign of infinity: ∞. The law runs out so far and then it begins to run itself into the other law, which runs so far and then runs itself into the other law, which runs into the other law. It becomes intertwined like a figure eight. If we could extrapolate that line and look at it under a microscope, we wouldn't see a straight line. We would see it twisting and turning in such a way that we could never find its ending or beginning. If you take this type of line dynamic and stretch it out as far as you can, you have a vortex.

The mystical writer has given us a new law. Basically, it is the law that "like <u>produces</u> like," and it's something we must not ignore. This is actually the Law of Cause and Effect. We are dealing with a law of action and life (cause and effect) without a number yet.

And the earth brought forth vegetation, the herb yielding seed after its kind, and the tree bearing fruit, wherein is its seed, after its kind; and God saw that it was good.

Genesis 1:12

The writer establishes the law to *Let there be* . . . Here is the law: *And God said, Let the earth bring forth vegetation, the herb yielding seed after its kind, and the fruit tree yielding fruit after its kind, wherein is their seed, upon the earth; and it was so.* From here, the natural progression is the action that followed: *And the earth brought forth vegetation, the herb yielding seed after its kind, and the tree bearing fruit, wherein is its seed, after its kind; and God saw that it was good.*

And there was evening and there was morning, the third day.

Genesis 1:13

We must not go beyond the event of the Law of Cause and Effect yet. Are we correct that the esoteric value of the number 3 is cause and effect, or should it be the Law of Creation? It doesn't make any difference whether the esoteric meaning of the number 3 is called "creation" or whether it's called "cause and effect" because those are identical terms. You cannot create without a cause and an effect, and you don't have a cause and an effect without having created. We often use the terminology Law of Creation or Law of Creative Force primarily because the word "creation," seems to be a better communicative term than the words "cause and effect."

There is an interesting relationship between the numbers 1, 2, and 3. The number 1 is an indivisible point in that it is total and complete. When we divide 1 by separating it down the center, we develop 2. Once we have 2, how do we progress from 2 to 3? If I have 2 pieces and I divide 1 of the pieces, I now have 3. However, if I put the 3 pieces I have separated back together, I have 1 again. 1 still existed in these three pieces. In terms of how 3 of anything exists, you cannot have 2 of anything without something happening in terms of interaction. Since the number 2 symbolizes separation, it produces a cause and an effect. As cause and an effect are produced, a third piece is formulated by some means because the number 3 symbolizes the thing that's being formulated. Two parts will never, ever stand still at zero because there will always be reflection. That reflection alone is interaction, and the interaction of reflection between the two parts that have been separated from the 1 produces 3.

If I say, "I observe one piece, and I observe another piece that is two pieces, but that is all I observe." The wise man comes along and says, "Please observe what goes on between one and two." I look down and say, "Oh, I see something." And he says, "Then don't you have three, and is not the third piece that you have exactly equaled to one and two?" Of course it is. Three is produced out of one and two, and whatever is happening between one and two is exactly equal to one and two because the reflection between the two pieces is exactly equal to one and two. If you take any type of triangle, that triangle can always be reconstructed to be exactly equal. It is always potentially equal. The triangle is the most powerful symbol in mysticism because, geometrically speaking, it combines the whole meaning of the esoteric laws of one, two, and three or the essence of the numbers 1, 2, and 3. There are many words to describe the triangle, but the most important indicators for it in mysticism are the beginning (1), separation (2), and creation (3). Because it's a symbol that includes these elements, the triangle always represents the total symbol of creation.

$1 + 2 = 3$, whether we are talking about reflection, length of line, or time and distance. It makes no difference. This all can be brought back into equal balance, which is extremely important because it is the lack of awareness that causes you to see an imbalance anywhere in your life. What has happened is that you've taken one, and you have split it. There is then one line, and there is another. You have made a mistake in assuming that the second line is greater than what it is, so you take an inaccurate view. You tell yourself that you are short of knowledge, money, friends, awareness, or whatever the lack appears to be. The mistake is that you have an imbalance between one and the other. You need to recognize what you are doing and correct yourself. Observe that the length of the third line that is the reflection between two lines is exactly what it should be in terms of cause and effect. The point of reflection is exactly equal to one and two.

The error is in your misinterpretation that one of these lines, as you view it, appears to be much longer than the other one. You must keep all these lines equal in using the law, whatever the length. They have to be of equal length so that whatever is going on between them is equal to the right and the left, the A and the B, the one and the two. This is why you look at your life and say that it's unfulfilled in some area, when in fact it is fulfilled. Let's put this into practical terms: A person has $500 of bills to pay in a one-month period. He says that he doesn't have enough money to pay his bills. We sit him down and ask him how much money he does have. He says that he has $200. We then ask why he's looking at the $500 debt when he has enough to take care of $200 of debt. He must cut the lines down to be equal by paying the $200, which is his creative effort. If he looks at the longer line, indicated by the $500 debt, he's looking at what he sees as lack. He should take the $200 and pay the debt. Doing so is the creative action of cause and effect and produces the other $300 along the way to give him a new line to pay the next $300. This is the effect in practical terms.

The person who says that he doesn't have the answer to a difficult research problem and is overwhelmed is doing exactly the same thing. He has let one of the lines go completely out of proportion. He should say, "This much of the problem I can keep in balance, and I'll let this much give me my creative effect, my cause and effect." It can be the smallest thing. It's like looking at a package of flower seeds. You can't see the flowers in the seeds. You've got to put it in its right perspective, which is nothing more than digging a hole in the ground, putting in the seeds, covering them up, and watering them. You hope that they're going to come up as flowers. Initially, the seeds disappear, but this is the only logical step in the growth and creativity of the plants.

This is a good lesson because many times you must bury and obliterate what you have in order to let it grow into what you need. The man who needs another $300 has to bury the $200 in equality in order to grow the other $300 he owes. He has to get the creative force going. Otherwise, he gets nothing. He stands around and keeps talking lack. This goes all the way back to reflection. This happens as the continuum of something that was wrong way back in the beginning that still needs rebalancing. Other people who scream about what you owe elongate one of the lines, which means that you look at their screaming as a reality. Is it a reality? Not really, if you understand the law. If you see it as a reality, it is because your reflection is wrong.

The quickest way to understand this is to admit that in order to do the proper job, the length of the lines must be kept equal. This admission will reposition you by extending these lines of their own accord. Creativity extends the lines, allowing you to take on a larger proportion, which extends the lines to take on a still larger proportion. One thing leads to another, and each thing extends the lines further and further so that the scope of personal activity can expand. This is true in everyone's life. You can see it in terms of your own life activity. The more you do, the more you find available to do within the scope of what you can do.

As long as these lines remain equal ("lines" meaning anything in your life be it money, friends, ideas, ad infinitum) so that you observe and produce the creative effort that's exactly equal, you are producing three (cause and effect). This will constantly bring the next logical step, much like it's written in the Story of Infinity in terms of *Let there be . . .* You have given direction by following the law. Every cause must have an effect. It has to happen; that is universal. You might ask, "Does that statement constitute faith?" I suppose so, but it is faith in the law not faith in a god with a long, white beard. It is faith in the law that says the Universe has never given me any reason to believe that It will deny Itself or destroy Itself or go against Itself in any way shape or form. I have every reason to believe that following the law will produce the next logical result. If I really need something strong to reinstitute the thought in my mind or to revitalize my eyes, I can always go back and read the Story of Infinity and see how many times God said, *Let there be* . . . And, if He can do it, whatever He might be, I guess I can do it.

The way the world is designed to operate is contained in the esoteric meaning, the essence, of the numbers 1, 2, and 3. In other words, 1, 2, and 3 are a unit unto themselves because they contain the basic elements of creation. We are now going to deal with a whole new aspect of Planet Earth.

This now completes the third day.

Discussion Questions

Why is it impossible to separate yourself from the Universe?

How can you create balance and harmony in your life?

What is the basic law of life on Planet Earth?

What does the Law of Karma mean?

What is the esoteric meaning of the number 3?

What is the quickest way to identify and correct an imbalance?

Why can't we help one another begin something?

Is it true that the more you do, the more opportunities become available to you?

What comes before the first day of creation and before the number 1?

Why are the numbers 1, 2, and 3 considered a unit unto themselves?

FOUR

The Construction of Planet Earth

Then God said, Let there be lights in the firmament of the heaven to separate the day from the night; and let them be for signs, and for seasons, and for days, and years.

Genesis 1:14

You have learned that the Universe doesn't leave anything up to chance. Everything was prepared for the establishment and birth of Planet Earth. There are herbs growing herbs, trees growing trees, and fruits growing fruits. As you expand your thinking, don't let yourself jump ahead. All events that are operating harmoniously also operate logically and sequentially within the basic components of an event. Those basic components are *the beginning,* which is based on the following:

- the five Prime Laws of Manifestation symbolized by the number 1
- the separation for the birth of the planet symbolized by the number 2
- the creation, which is the Law of Cause and Effect or the Law of Karma, symbolized by the number 3

What's important to you as the reader is that the Story of Infinity is now going on with other laws, other directions, and other answers. Up to now, you've been told how the space was prepared for the birth of the planet, how the planet was born, and what the basic characteristics are that will govern its entire lifetime. Now, the mystical writers are establishing the elements of how you are going to get along here. Mind you, human beings have not arrived yet as you and I like to think of human beings.

The word *Then* indicates an absolute change in the energy frequency of the story; *Then* stops the forward movement and starts a vortical movement. This is another dimension. Up to now, the writer has used the connector *and* to indicate continuity and to produce a certain picture. Remember to be aware of these connector words as you go along. Also with this kind of an abrupt shift, you must understand that there is a new mystical writer. He is getting down to the nitty-gritty of how we are going to exist on this planet.

What kind of meaning is attached to *Then God said*? In terms of the first day, the second day, and the third day, it means that 1, 2, and 3 are considered a basic unit. This is why the triangle, as a three-sided symbol, is considered the most powerful of symbols in mysticism. It geometrically and esoterically symbolizes the beginning (1), the separation (2), and the creation (3).

Then God said, Let there be lights in the firmament of the heaven to separate the day from the night. The writer must be telling you something different because day and night have already been separated. This time, he's telling you about the *lights in the firmament.* You've already learned that *the firmament* means the vortex of energy and how it operates, so something is happening with the energy. You can read it to mean this: Let there be action in the energy of the heaven to separate the day from the night. However, that doesn't make sense because there has already been a separation. The mystic gives you the next logical step by going with this explanation: *and let them be for signs, and for seasons, and for days, and years.* He is telling you that the action that takes place in the energy has nothing to do with the separation of day and night but with a more technical situation: *for signs.*

And let them be for signs is a very important consideration. We have a solar system, and we have planets moving around the sun. One of the most basic life sciences is the observation of the solar system, the science of astronomy. By observing the solar system, we learn how to better understand the place of Planet Earth and its importance in relationship to everything else in the solar system. Scientifically speaking, this gives you your first open window to the Universe. The door to the Universe, from where we are, is the solar system and the observation of movements within the solar system.

In any kind of science, you learn through the construction of some kind of symbols. Mathematics is the construction of symbols for signs. You have a known point and an unknown point. The known point allows you to put in what is known to solve what is unknown. You then proceed to the next unknown; signs point to signs, and symbols point to symbols. In this first part of separation with energy, the writer means for you to establish a science of *the heaven*, which is the science of astronomy and its sister, astrology. As you learn about the science of our own solar system, you learn more in universal terms. You know more because we can get to the moon and can observe from that point, just as we know more because we can send a camera to Mars. We no longer see Planet Earth as flat.

The first action of energy, after the basic unit of 1, 2, and 3, was to establish a science for this planet. Our solar system is the science for Earth, for Mars, and for all the planets and stars. Obviously, Planet Earth is not separated from the solar system. It's divided but it's not separated. In relationship, it's in balance to all the other planets in the same way that you might have seven people in your family. You can measure the harmony, disharmony, or the condition of the family by measuring each individual in the family as a single unit. We cannot understand Planet Earth by just looking at it all by itself because it has a relationship to all other planets in the solar system. The whole idea is for you to know where you are and where you are going. Within our current time, both astronomy and astrology are still in their infancy.

You now know that *let them be for signs* means the establishment of these actions was for signs or science in any form. The writer continues with *and for seasons, and for days, and years*. The progression of science is related to the cycles of science, the cycles of the earth, the cycles of the solar system, and the cycles of mankind. Advancement in everything is cyclic. The seasons, the days, the months, and the year are nothing more than the cyclic situation that was set up initially by activating a heavenly energy force to produce these two results. This is an interesting picture. Let your mind be receptive for a moment.

There is an ancient and ongoing mystical discussion that comes out of this: *lights in the firmament of the heaven* means action into the energy of heaven that produces a science that further produces cycles. To take this into the largest extension of its probability, you might say that when Planet Earth was formed there was formation of many of the planets also, if not all of them. Conceivably, this solar system was formed all at once, and there's no difference in actual age between Earth, Mars, Jupiter, and all the other planets. Out of this one statement comes a very conceivable, logical, and infinite argument for this solar system being formed all at once because the establishment was there in space. The law applying here could well apply to all other planets in the solar system. While I, Gregge, cannot prove this, I am laying out the argument because (in mystical terms) my teachers and I (and others) have gone into great depth in trying to either prove it or disprove that line. The further you go into it, the more unlikely you are to prove it. Nevertheless, there's an infinite capability of this being a very real and true possibility.

As writers change, frequencies change, and we even change geographical position. You are told that signs and cycles have been established. This leads one to believe that, in mystical terms, *of the heaven* doesn't relate to Planet Earth's heaven but rather is a term that means "space." Heaven could well be a logical basis for understanding how the solar system was established as one unit at one time and that the law that applies here could also well apply to all other points in this solar system.

What you are meant to do is to take cycles, which is not time (man makes time and the Universe works in cycles), and start proving the whole meaning of cycles as established in heaven. When you do this, the first thing you realize is that time has very little association to this planet because the whole solar system is operating in cyclic systems. We know through astronomy (and its sister astrology) that planets have very definitive pathways. We can chart these pathways to produce a whole cyclical picture of the solar system. Is the mystical writer really trying to tell us about the formation of Planet Earth as nothing more than a focus story about the whole formation of the solar system? He has been telling you, all the way up to this point, about the establishment of this planet. Then suddenly, he stops the story and throws it into a complex solar system.

Regardless of whether you are proving or disproving that the solar system was born as a single unit all at the same time, you do know that there's something very important here which cannot be ignored. That is that you are subject to the observation of the science of cycles. What does this mean to you and me because we have to live here? It means exactly what it says. We've got to look at the science of cycles as it pertains to us. What is the science of cycles as it pertains to us? It is nothing more than observing our cycles from beginning to separation to creation. Creation on Planet Earth is a <u>manifested</u> end, and once manifested, the creation is finished.

It's true that people overwork creation. A painter finishes his painting, and then he ruins it rather than blessing it, and leaving it alone. In the same way, the writer writes another ending or writes another word instead of leaving the manuscript as is. Observing the science of cycles is the individual's most important act of creation: the beginning, the separation, and the cause and effect (which is the actual creation). Anything that goes through a beginning, a weighing and balancing (separation), and a manifestation (cause and effect) is a completed cycle. A cycle can be short or long. It can be anything that incorporates these three elements.

Now you can see why this mystical writer, in terms of sequence, stopped everything in the story. He wanted you to know emphatically that the key to life (other than the use and formation of these laws) is your ability to do whatever it takes to sequentially go through steps one, two, and three. Seasons, days, weeks, and months are the science of cycles or the science of creation. The Universe didn't develop birth and death. It doesn't even know death, and It doesn't really know birth. In the beginning when all of this was taking place to prepare the place in space, it was not the very first time that this happened. It was the continuum of something you know nothing about. The mystic starts his story in the middle of something that you know nothing about, which lets you rightly assume that there's another story before and beyond this one that tells you something else. Therefore, the better word for "death" is "creation" because death does not end anything. It creates in light of what the beginning wanted to create in the beginning.

There's always a point of creation from which you move on to the next beginning of the next creation. The beginning meets the creation, and the creation meets the beginning. You've got to know when you have created, and that is that. One of the biggest blocks in simply living on this planet is to know when you've created not when you've finished. "Finished" leads you to believe that there's an end, but nothing has an end point. In other words, there is no space in your vocabulary for E-N-D. There is no end; world without end. Amen. When you are operating within the law, you are in total control. The situation does not control you; you control the situation. Your growth is predicated upon seeing and applying the science of cycles, not simply upon beginning; weighing and balancing; and creating—as wonderful as those three steps may be.

Take, for example, the association between two people. It's the most ongoing form of beginning, separation, and creation, whether you're creating attitudes, ideas, or babies. The process is ongoing and works from these cycles all the time. You never finish eating, you never finish sleeping, and you never finish exercising. One thing leads to another. You don't finish anything, and this is what's so important in the science of cycles. You never establish A as a beginning and X as an end. The universal law does not apply in that direction. The universal law says you establish A (a beginning). The thing you're concerned with next is the separation, and the only thing you're concerned with after that is the creation. When you arrive at the creation, the next beginning will be obvious to you. It doesn't constitute an end to anything.

If you want to say that A is the beginning and X is the creation, you can say that. But, why jump one step? The second step is essential to life on this planet. You look from 1 to 2 to 3, not from 1 to 3. After all of this has been done and the beginning is established, you're aware because the last point is finite awareness. You're going to be aware of whatever is separated because separation gives you something to weigh and balance in terms of handling the two separated pieces. The two separated pieces then rush together, reflecting off of each other to form the triangulation, the creation, from your effort.

You're always moving toward a constant form of creation but not toward a goal as an end point. Creation produces the next beginning to the next creation. You then look at your life and say, "I am not living to accomplish. I am living to create, and I am living to begin." When the cycle moves from beginning through separation and to creation, it closes itself and expands to the next cycle. We have a vortex spiraling onward, outward, and upward. Fortunately, your awareness of yourself progresses from a beginning to a creation to your next beginning. However, you cannot arrive at creation only to recognize that there's something that needs to be corrected. Otherwise, you have not arrived at the point of creation yet. You are still getting there.

The writer is telling you that you must deal with this as a science of living. You must deal with it as the only thing that's important in terms of <u>your</u> observation in a scientific way, and he means scientific. What constitutes a scientific action on Planet Earth? Nothing more than the logical orientation of signs that provides points along the way that give you enough basic interior intelligence to know how you got to that creation and to know where you are along the way. The science of cycles is the science of awareness. It's to know when you have arrived and to feel free to go on from there to the next logical step. It's like the connector in the story: *and God said, and God saw, and God made.*

And let them be for lights in the firmament of the heaven to give light upon the earth; and it was so.

Genesis 1:15

To give light upon the earth means to give action upon the earth. The mystic is carrying on with the science of cycles. In the next verse, he writes:

And God made two great lights, the greater light to rule the day, and the smaller light to rule the night; and the stars also.

Genesis 1:16

Since *light* is action, the writer is indicating that there will be a cycle when activity is greater and another cycle of lesser activity. We know it as awake and asleep, but the words "awake" and "asleep" never appear in the story. You just have to know that the greater and lesser awareness of the science of cycles is what is meant by *the greater light* and *the smaller light.*

And God set them in the firmament of the heavens to give light upon the earth.

Genesis 1:17

And to rule over the day and over the night, and to separate the light from the darkness; and God saw that it was good.

Genesis 1:18

What we have here is the continuation of the writer's concept of what is necessary for approval.

And there was evening and there was morning, the fourth day.

Genesis 1:19

You are now into the fourth element, the fourth day. You've learned that *signs* are symbols organized in a logical order leading you from that which is known to that which is unknown, so you can solve that which is unknown in order to know. Therefore, everything that precedes the action of the fourth day pertains to the establishment of signs (science), which aren't disorganized as we know them. Obviously then, the esoteric meaning of four is the observation of the science of cycles or the observation of creation.

In esoteric terms, the number 4 is the assigned number of the planet, but it's been misused and misinterpreted. It's the assigned number for Earth because it's the first number that actually addresses the lifestyle of the planet in terms of the science of cycles. However, as a result of misinterpretation, people have built everything in squares. This is absolutely wrong and is holding people back. The reason that people have built everything in squares is because squares have two sides that are equal. That looks nice and organized, but it defeats the science of cycles because a cycle runs in a vortex, which is a cylindrical motion.

Actually, the most logical way to build on this planet is triangular. The planet, if not the whole universe, is basically crystalline. In every crystal, you can see the triangles. The pyramids are the perfect harmonious structure for this plane. The geodesic dome is another example where combinations of triangles are put together to form a larger element that is still triangular in its totality. It is made up of an infinite number of triangles over a given space. All elements fit on triangular pieces to form a circular dome. The geodesic dome is a perfect building pattern for this planet. It's an example of the science of observation: symbols all lined up in their proper order leading to a proper creation. You'd experience a most marked change in well-being, with a general feeling of expansive intelligence, if you would lived and worked in triangular buildings rather than in squares. Consciousness, by virtue of its constant base unit of triangulation, would find itself expanding its limits without any outside irritations.

This is why society is so square. You live in square buildings. You have square attitudes about everything, and you really don't have a sense of expansiveness. You think and live in very, very limited ways because you are so used to the limitations of the square, which are not in harmony with the way the planet is set up. Individuals who lived in igloos and American Indians who lived in cone-shaped teepees lived closer to the reality of nature and to universal law. They were fully educated to their own needs and their own way of life.

If I were to put you in a triangular-shaped room that was completely mirrored, it would blast you so far out in consciousness that you might not be able to get back into your body. It would absolutely explode you because there'd be no point in the room where there wasn't a reflection. The first thing that would happen is that consciousness would immediately, by its own accord, bang out as fast and as far as it could because of the reflection of energy. You couldn't come out sane as we know it. In a matter of milliseconds, consciousness would blow completely out of the physical vehicle's limitations. It would drive you wild even within a perfect triangle made of stone. Such an experience can be very negative as well as positive. You cannot stand the sense of vibration going on. That is why the pyramids were built the way they were. The idea of the construction was to speed the consciousness of the departed heavenward by blasting it free from the earth. The pyramids are really a space station. Also, limestone has a very deep vibration. I have now given you enough information about triangulation to drive you crazy, so this is as far as we are going to go with it.

And God said, Let the waters bring forth swarms of living creatures, and let fowl fly above the earth in the open firmament of the heaven.

Genesis 1:20

The writer is now going through the construction of Planet Earth along with the new laws regarding how the planet is to operate. He writes, *And God said, Let the waters . . .,* and we know that *let* indicates God didn't do anything. This is the next natural progression for the planet: *Let the waters bring forth swarms of living creatures, and let fowl fly above the earth.* Obviously, out of the *waters* (out of the spirituality) of the planet is born your first element in terms of *creatures. Waters* is the first key word that you want to consider because your mind, operating on basic human elements, understands that life comes from the sea. However, life cannot come from the sea because you can turn around and ask, "How did life get in the sea? What in the water produced the life?" These are not unanswerable questions. If life came from the sea or from a drop of water, how did the life force, the microcosm, or whatever you want to call it, get there? The answer is that water cannot be construed in literal terms.

What does *living creatures* mean? At this point, for all you're concerned with, *creatures* can mean anything that's living. And, you can rightly assume that *let fowl fly above the earth in the open firmament of the heaven* means that the flying element came as a natural growth factor out of creatures. You have a tadpole, and then you have a frog. In the natural progression of life on the planet (coming out of the spiritual form), there was probably a basic elemental form of some sort. From creatures, fowl were developed. There is a link of genetic progression that takes place. That's important because it helps teach you that Planet Earth and its elements were not just thrown together. Everything is still working according to the blueprint as planned.

And God created great sea monsters, and every living creature that moves, which the waters brought forth abundantly after their kind, and every winged fowl after its kind; and God saw that it was good.

Genesis 1:21

The first time *created* was used in Genesis 1:1, it meant that the story about to be told was a story that has been told in its realistic existence, and we are just carrying on with it. Now, even after four major laws and a multitude of natural progressions of the planet (including its early preparation in space and the conceivability and possibility that the solar system may have been born all at the same time), the word *created* has not been used again.

And God created great sea monsters is only the second time that the word *created* has been used. If looked at literally, this is a statement that is all wrong. *God created the heavens and the earth in the very beginning* means there was an established order of infinity in existence. There was always creation. The next step in the progression is the Story of Infinity (Genesis), and that's very important because it pertains to our particular planet. We cannot look at *And God created great sea monsters* without asking ourselves if God can create twice when everything has already been created. That is redundant. The fact is, in the beginning there was creation, and that leads us to believe there was always creation. Our antenna should be ringing bells all over the place when we find the word *created* for the second time. God can't create on creation. We don't create on creation. When we create, all we are doing is carrying on an existing process.

Do you ever create an original thought, an original painting, an original automobile, or an original anything? Of course you don't. You're just carrying on a continual process of flow, which you've come to see throughout this story in almost everything. All you're doing is uncovering a significant point that you can look at and then extrapolate, if you like, the natural outgrowth from the point just before it, which came from the point just before that. If you sat for billions of years and asked that question, you would still be going back and back and back never to find the beginning. Therefore, you cannot create anything new because you cannot create upon creation especially in the mystical sense. It cannot be done.

Since God cannot create twice, the writer has to mean something else. Everything that has been created has already been created, so *created* cannot mean "new." It has to mean "progression," but what else does *And God created* prepare us for? Doesn't infinity indicate that something already exists and has existed and ever will exist? The writer is telling you that the existence of whatever is going to be created here has already existed. God didn't develop the Master Plan. *God*, as the term is being used here, is only acting as the natural passageway, the natural medium, for something that already exists in the universe. This proves something that science is still afraid to look at but has been trying to prove for hundreds of years: There might be other creatures and other types of creation exactly like ours in the universe. Obviously, this is not an original model. This is the answer that science is looking for, in the terms of possibility, even though it doesn't prove anything and would not be accepted on scientific terms. However, it certainly opens the doors of probability if you understand what the writer is talking about.

Creation indicates infinity of action; therefore, whatever is going to be created here is the ongoing plan of a Master Plan. There must be the possibility of something very similar (though not identical because the Universe doesn't repeat Itself) to this kind of procedure elsewhere that produces a very parallel existence.

Artists act as mediums between the thought process and manifestation by seeing in the mind's eye that which they've already looked at in some way, often called imagination. If an artist wants to do a painting of a three-headed man with three ears, you know that the artist must be looking at something because nothing can be invented or created that has not already been created. This proves that consciousness isn't limited to the physical confines of your body or to whatever it sees. It's limited only by what the Universe is willing to show it in terms of Its own will to look at something. Now, we are getting a bigger and bigger picture. It's the will of the Universe to be infinite.

When you're creative, it defines one more aspect of the universal reality. The universal reality is that all things that are to be created have been created. It's like the more rocks you turn over, the more bugs you find underneath them. Don't you see what this means on a personal level?

You don't have to worry about your definition, in terms of where you're going or what you have to do. All you have to do is to open up the eyes of your consciousness, realizing that you are the medium or the tool of an unlimited Universe, which allows you an infinite amount of expression. Creativity is simply a matter of making a choice at any given moment. You choose, in the infinity of the Universe, to extrapolate that point and put it inside your life as an experience. You make a choice. You can make a choice here or down the road because you're constantly making choices along the way.

Creative effort (or creation) does not exist outside the confines of natural progression. For the sake of playing around with words, "second creation" cannot create until there's a beginning, separation, creation, and organization. Then, you can find the elements to define the esoteric value of the fifth day. However, you cannot skip over the word *created* and just assume that God created again. Your mind needs to take an enormous leap in order to find out that God created nothing. He did nothing more, in the terms of the writer, than to establish the fact that the Universe (in Its progression) is preparing to bring into the action of this planet something that obviously exists in the Master Plan. Since it appears in the Master Plan, it could well have a parallel or sister action somewhere else in the universe. While the action is not identical, it's certainly not without some parallel. If you can deal with *creatures* here, then you must be able to deal with creatures someplace else. You might say in scientific terms that this is a weak argument for life somewhere else in the universe. That is, if you add all the other esoteric knowledge you can compile with this Story of Infinity, you can draw some parallels for yourself. Now let's see what happens in the progression.

The action in *And God said, Let the waters bring forth swarms of living creatures, and let fowl fly above the earth in the open firmament of the heaven* indicates issuing forth of the swarms of living creatures from the earth itself. The earth is

THE CONSTRUCTION OF PLANET EARTH   85

birthing its own natural progression as its natural function. In other words, creatures and birds are the natural outpouring of the planet's character and its functions.

And God created great sea monsters, and every living creature that moves, which the waters brought forth abundantly after their kind, and every winged fowl after its kind indicates that from the Universal action, or impregnation, developed a group of large sea (spirituality) monsters. The progression is not earth action by itself. Great spirituality (consciousness) enters from the waters (from the Universe), and as a result of once entering, consciousness then produces from itself. In other words, the Universe gives, and that which It gives, gives back to It. Unless consciousness arrives from its Universal Source, there is no such thing as human birth. Before the fetus, there is consciousness.

The manifestation of man has not occurred yet. Up to now, this is the regurgitation of the goods of the earth and the infusion of the goods from the Universe. It is the intercourse of the earth to the Universe and the Universe to the earth, with consciousness playing its basic role. *Great sea monsters* indicates an ongoing act of the Universe acting upon the planet. Alarm bells should be going off inside of you. *Monsters* is plural, which can mean hundreds, hundreds of thousands, or a hundred million because the mystic is talking in huge terms. This is very important. It's very important that you see this as the action from the Universe to make sure that the writer knows what he's talking about. If he had written, "and God created a great sea monster," you'd have to say that something is wrong. Either the story has been misprinted, or the writer doesn't know what he's talking about because universal action is never singular. You are looking for this hallmark of plurality to make sure that the universal actions of multiplicity, duality, and infinity are upheld and sustained.

You also have to define a key element. *Great* is a non-word. You don't know how great because it has to be comparative. *Great* might mean size, or energy, or it might have some other defining quality but not right now. You don't know—yet.

What do you have when you get to sea? You know that water is a symbol for spirituality, but you need to consider the different characteristics between a sea and a stream. Do not complicate this comparison. A stream is generally small. It isn't very deep, and its power is somewhat limited by its size; it changes direction quite often; it cannot sustain a great deal of life, and it can get clogged from leaves falling in it. These are simple, knowable, general facts. A sea is large, enormous, and deep. It hides a lot of light in it, and it's powerful. Water is a symbol of spirituality, so it can be a lot of things and can go into a lot of areas as a symbol for spirituality. The writer used sea as *great sea monsters*. In terms of definition, he is trying to get across to you, in terms of the action of the Universe upon the planet, that *sea* has something to do with power, greatness, depth, majesty, and tremendous mystery. Even with modern technology, it's hard to go into the sea and know all there is to know about it. Now, the phrase is beginning to make some sense.

And God created great sea monsters. The Universe is acting upon the planet in spiritual, powerful, enormous magnitude. With that in mind, the writer used *great* to enhance the symbolism of the sea. He had to use *monsters*. The mystic wasn't taking any chances that the mystical student (who should know what he is talking about at this point) would be confused or would misunderstand that what was being done to the earth by the Master Plan was far greater and enormously greater in scope than the earth bringing forth a swarm of creatures. *Great sea monsters* comes from the strongest spiritual element that he could put in here as the ultimate symbol of spirituality.

This is why you see so many stories about the sea in the New Testament. There was a storm while Jesus and the fishermen were at sea. There is the baptismal at the sea and Jesus walking on the sea. This is why the sea is used as an expression of spirituality for Planet Earth. It is the highest symbolic level of spirituality. The writer wanted to be sure that he followed this up with *monsters* — something you could not conceivably miss. In any terminology, a monster is something bigger than life, far above *creatures*. There is a degree of ugliness to the word, which is unnecessary in terms of what the writer is trying to tell us. He's emphasizing that it is a size far beyond what we would normally expect as belonging to the planet according to what the planet would bring forth.

The planet does not bring forth monsters. The Universe brings forth monsters. The planet brings forth swarms of creatures. Now we know what is happening.

And God created great sea monsters, and every living creature that moves, which the waters brought forth abundantly after their kind, and every winged fowl after its kind; and God saw that it was good. The Universe has acted upon the earth at its point of greatest spirituality to bring forth the largest conceivable effect. It's obvious that the action of the Universe upon the planet is to magnify in size or to reintroduce the infinity of life upon the planet.

The planet gives birth out of its own natural resources, but the Universe gave the initial life force to begin with, instead of saying, "There you are. We'll just hang around and see what happens." What would happen? Life would die. Life could not be sustained, so the Universe acts upon the earth to magnify the life force. After this is done, the next most logical step is for the earth to issue forth another birth, and the Universe acts upon that and magnifies it. There you have the whole system of life like an accordion moving outward, inward, outward, inward. There is the whole breath and heartbeat of life on the planet.

You cannot turn around and ask what the meaning of life is because the writer has now given you the key to life. It simply boils down to this: All First Cause comes from the Universe, and you don't ask what First Cause is since you've learned that the Universe has already established First Cause. Out of First Cause comes your action no matter how infinitesimal. It might be a word or whatever, but as soon as your action manifests, the Universe acts upon it to give a magnified scope for that action. This universal magnification gives you the ability to put out another action, perhaps larger. It is a basic sub-law that the more you do, the more the Universe supports what you do. For example, I'm putting out an action to tell you what I think I know. When you act upon it, there is a greater action. There is a certain energy that occurs as a result of energy acting upon itself growing larger and larger and larger.

To sustain the law of the Universe's own infinity, the Universe must magnify our actions. If you were to produce no action, you would give the Universe nothing to magnify, and the initial action out of the earth would die. It could not sustain itself. What would it use to sustain itself? You do not live by yourself alone. You live by the grace of the Universe interacting with you. Therefore, if you sit and vegetate and do nothing, you offer nothing for the Universe to act upon. The destruction of life is apathy, not to do. What's the best advice to follow when your psychological level is low? Good advice is to do something because any action will be acted upon, not by your fellow man or by the earth, but by the natural action of the Universe. The Universe magnifies your effort.

We are not talking about whether you have the technique or technology. We are talking about just doing something so the Universe can work upon your actions. The basic law of life is to put out energy so that the Universe can act upon your actions and magnify them so you can put out more energy. This can be used in a negative sense also. This is how you get the rabble going. This is how Hitler and others like him, who preceded him and came after him, instituted activity. The Universe does not know. It's just acting according to infinite law. The Universe can only act on Its whole. It receives an action, and It acts on the action. If the action is to get 100,000 people to run roughshod over a town with the outpouring of all the energy, which is action, the Universe gives support for it. It cannot and does not discern whether or not that is a "good" action.

A writer who struggles for years and years and is penniless comes to mind. Finally, he writes a great novel and becomes an overnight success. His consistent action of writing increased the momentum, and finally at the right point (whatever that might mean to the Universe), he issues forth the child of all of his efforts. The Universe looks at all the action and bang! There is the magnification. See what's going on? What you need to be aware of in using the law is that it's up to you to get the *swarms of living creatures* out. It's up to you to *let fowl fly* on a <u>consistent</u> basis so the Universe can magnify your actions without overwhelming you. Do people generally do this? No, the actions are usually erratic, so the Universe, trying to work on Its magnification, simply cannot work on erratic lines. The Universe works on consistency.

You do not know how strong the effect is going to be. An artist doesn't know how good his painting really is until he paints it and gets it out. The Universe cannot magnify it if you stick it in the closet. How do you know the manuscript isn't that good? How do you know you can't sing? How do you know you don't have a great idea? You have to get it out because it has to work within the confines of the law. The law says you have got to issue it forth from the planet and allow the Universe to work back on it in magnified terms. This is the Law of Cause and Effect in operation because whatever you give birth to at this point, the magnification will be exactly that thing. If this point is evil, the magnification will be the magnification of evil. The Universe cannot see its parts. It only acts upon Its normal body as a totality.

Look at your surroundings. It's hardly practical for you to go live on a mountaintop. Analyze what you are giving birth to. If you have an intelligent mind trained to do certain technical things, you wouldn't bury it. The obvious thing to do is use it in that category. If you have musical talent, you want to be able to express it, so sit down and play. People are too concerned about what is "good," which defeats the law. Saying, "I am good at this," doesn't have anything to do with the whole scope of the system any more than "great" does.

Great is just the writer's way of telling you, without any mistake, what large magnification means. The only way you get good is to practice. Everyone who is really good at something trains and trains and trains. What does that training amount to? Learning is a secondary issue.

Training amounts to giving birth to that which you can do so the Universe can add to it and magnify the effort. With that kind of continuity, you become good, if not great. The same way that you differentiate between a meal that sets well and one that brings indigestion is the same way with the Universe. It senses on an intelligent level. The Universe cannot magnify what is unsettled.

You have a responsibility to recognize the Law of Cause and Effect. By putting this material into use, you must be responsible for its validity and its spiritual value. The Universe is going to act upon what you do no matter what. The Universe will act upon it at the greatest degree of spiritual effect. That is the law of motion, the law of life, the law of energy, and the law of karma, all of which mean the same thing.

This is the construction of Planet Earth.

Discussion Questions

What was the first <u>action</u> of energy after the basic unit of 1, 2, and 3 was established?

What is the difference between man-made time and universal cycles?

How can you know when you're finished with a creative project?

How do you progress from what you know to what you don't know?

What is the esoteric meaning of the number 4?

What gives your life definition?

What does natural progression have to do with creative effort?

Do you believe that universal energy acts upon what you do?

Why can't the Universe magnify inconsistency?

What are you birthing?

FIVE

The Mandate

And God blessed them, saying, Be fruitful and multiply, and fill the waters in the seas, and let fowl multiply on the earth.

Genesis 1:22

What would happen if you painted a picture, and when it was completed, you blessed it? What is the action of *blessed*? Blessed is an approval, but is approval also considered judgment? I am the only one who has a right to judge my own efforts. Therefore, I am the only one who can issue an approval of my efforts. I'm not talking about approval coming from any place else. If the Universe didn't judge Itself, It wouldn't know when It's out of balance. What is true of the part is true of the whole, and everything is working on the line of infinity. Judgment isn't issued forth from you to something else, nor is it issued forth from the Universe to something outside Itself. That's impossible. Rather, judgment is issued forth from an individual to oneself. I have a right to judge, but the only right I have is to judge my own self or my own energy output.

In terms of seeing, you are observing a reflection, but the word "reflection" isn't a strong enough word to consider for *blessed*. Within all of the complexity we've talked about, self-judgment is the means by which you define and observe the points on the line. This indicates where you are in relation to the opposite polarities. This is a judgment. If I say, "I'm one foot away from one wall and twenty feet away from another wall," that's a judgment. If I say, "I am where I should be, and I approve of where I am," that is a judgment and an approval up to that point of identification. In other words, judgment is a relationship to the polarities at any given point.

At this point in the story, what is it that *God* has *blessed*? We have *fowl, winged fowl, creatures,* and we have *sea monsters*. All of these represent the issuing forth of creatures out of the earth and the universal reaction of magnification in terms of manifestation of the forms on the earth. *And God blessed them* is the totality of relationship. It is the whole outworking of the planet being right, the universal magnification being right, and the observation of the interaction between the outworking of the planet and the universal magnification being right. The significant point is the observation of those cycles. Therefore, a blessing is an approval of observation. An approval must include a judgment. What we have here is an individual's awareness (or self-judgment) of universal interaction with the planet.*

And God saw that it was good is the reflection. Now, He blesses the reflection, which is an approval to indicate (and incorporates within it) a judgment. When I <u>see</u> you, I can say that there is a reflection. However, all that means is what it means to me in terms of reflection. If I say, "You are good," or I use the word that is used here and I *bless* you, then I am making an approval. The approval isn't necessarily of you, but it's an approval of that reflection within me. It is twofold. You are on one end of the polarity, and I'm on the other end. If you approve of anything, you no longer hold on to it. For instance, a person who takes a canvas and doesn't bless it does not approve of it; he's not going to get rid of it. He's going to hold on to it. Artists who paint a lot but do not sell their paintings because they cannot part with them are telling us that they don't approve of what they've done. They've made a judgment, and their judgment is that the painting isn't as good as they want it to be or as good as they can do. Therefore, they can't get rid of it. Both approval and blessing come under the same heading.

Somewhere along the line in the mundane terms of our religious background, you've heard the expression, "May

---

**Into the Universe* in *The Collected Works of Gregge Tiffen* details macrocosm and microcosm principles.

God bless you." You're seeking God's approval as a result of that phraseology. It's understood (but not necessarily a stated attitude in your mind) that you are waiting for His approval. "May God bless you," means may God approve of what you are, who you are, where you are going, and what you are doing. The mystical writer indicates two very important aspects here. Judgment represents approval, and within approval is self-judgment. That judgment is born by reflection, which is already within the law by separation and creation; reflection comes out of the beginning.

The writer is telling you about the continuum of a very important action: an interaction between universal energy and earth energy that issues forth life. *And God blessed them* indicates that I observe, I reflect, I recognize, and I have awareness according to the Prime Laws of Manifestation: Sound, Direction, Reflection, Recognition, and Finite Awareness. Approval is a form of blessing for recognition and judgment. The phrase, "May God bless you," is really asking that He identify you and judge you good, or not good, but that He judge you and approve.

The initial picture is the earth issuing forth and the Universe acting upon that action of earth energy. The process goes on and on, which is the heartbeat and breath of life. You need to reach a point where you recognize approval. How are you going to recognize approval? The writer cannot leave you hanging in limbo. He recognizes that, at some point, you have to have a point of recognition. You've got to know what's going on, and you can only know what's going on by identifying where you stand in relation to the polarities that you can see.

Once you see the interaction of output and input happening and the enormous beauty of creation, your normal reaction is, "I approve." What you're actually saying is, "From my point of observation, I bless it." You are accustomed to judgment meaning something between good or bad, should or shouldn't, and right or wrong. Of course, judgment doesn't mean that. Judgment is reflected awareness by identifying a point and recognizing that point. You then know how far away you are from any polarity.

And God blessed them. The writer is trying to bring the lesson to you that, in order for this to be valuable to you, you must observe the interaction to find out where you are, and then to know where you are in relation to the two polarities that you can see. If you say that nothing is working out in your life, I can turn around and say to you that, based on what's being considered here, you're obviously not even aware or awake enough to see where you are. If you were, you would see that what's wrong with your life is that your output is either erratic or so little that the Universe can't magnify it properly. Therefore, you don't know where you are. And, if you don't know where you are, you can't approve of yourself. This is one of the biggest factors for people who are unhappy. They don't approve of themselves, and they don't bless themselves because they don't know where they are. This goes around and around in a circle.

There is a saying in metaphysics that leans heavily on blessing oneself. It's essential to understand the terminology. Blessing yourself is giving yourself approval but only <u>after</u> going through the process of observation on your reflection and recognizing where you are in relation to the polarities in order to have finite awareness. This includes a judgment, but the judgment is not about whether you are good or bad. Rather, it's about where you are in relation to the polarities of life. In totality, every time you bless and approve of yourself, you also bless the basic universal pulsating action of life expansion. You're saying to the Universe that you like your life and that the Universe is really doing a great thing. Of course, the Universe is working exactly as It should, whether or not you are aware of it. It's beneficial to you when you identify yourself and indicate approval. *And God blessed them* refers to the *fowl*, the *creatures*, and the *monsters* as the action of life and all of its parts.

And God blessed them, <u>saying</u>, . . . is a tremendous and overwhelmingly important point because it's only the second time that God has spoken. Up to now, God has only observed and not said anything since the very first verse where we read, *And God said,* followed by the word *Let,* which is the normal point of observation for further action. Now, we have, *And God blessed them, saying, Be fruitful and multiply. Be* is a mandate. It's an order; it's a direction with enormous significance.

What's the significance of God's mandate? After God approved of what He saw, He set in this mandate, which is saying that He sees what has happened in universal form. The earth issues forth from itself, and the Universe magnifies what the earth issues forth. The mandate is that you continue the Master Plan, that you go on with it, and that you do nothing to disrupt the flow. The mandate is that you shall be fruitful and multiply. What are you multiplying? You are multiplying the whole process of life.

The practical approach to this and the practical meaning this has for you is that you can't get something for nothing. You must act. There's a saying that goes, "Man proposes, and God disposes." This isn't a bad phrase, except instead of "God" disposing, use the term "Universe." Man acts. The Universe reacts adding to the initial action. Then, man approves of the action as a result of approval issuing forth the next mandate, which is basically to himself to continue the action.

If there's ever any question as to what life means, I don't know how it can be any clearer: The part can only know the part. You look at the polarities and say that you're in harmony with the polarities, which is just looking at another part. If you could look at the whole, you'd spend all of your time gazing at that fantastic view, but you know you can't see the whole. As close as you can come is the utter enjoyment of seeing the part, in its entirety, so you can approve of the part. That approval is self-approval. I bless me because I approve of where I am in my view. When that no longer satisfies me, then I act, the Universe reacts, which adds to me. I then change my position and move to a new point of approval, a point of new awareness and judgment.

That method, like a molecular structure, allows me to move from point to point to point, learning more and more, seeing more and more, and becoming more and more intimately satisfied with who I am. You never have to worry about the whole because you know, by the Law of Cause and Effect, that if you're putting forth a harmonious effort, the only thing that can be magnified is a harmonious effort. Therefore, the magnification of the effort is good. I know that if I stay within writing distance of a blackboard that I can continue my creative effort, and I know that I can't write on the blackboard from the back of the room. It's obvious that the most harmonious thing for me to do is to stay within arm's distance of the blackboard. That's so logical that it cannot be refuted.

The Universe will magnify whatever effort you put out because it can't identify that effort as good or bad, right or wrong. It only identifies your effort as energy. Electricity that comes into the building, in terms of its energy, does not know that it's giving us light. When you stick your finger in the electrical socket and electrocute yourself, the electricity doesn't know it's electrocuting you. It only knows that it's flowing. To whatever degree you accept, control, or react, the energy does exactly what you mandate.

You have to understand that that's such a beautiful thing about the Universe. You've got to become aware of that significance. Somewhere along the line, you have to sit down and realize that this whole massive thing (beyond your wildest vision) is all for you. It's not for us collectively. It's for you individually because collectively it doesn't mean anything. Individually, it means something. There's no one to really tell you what you can and can't do or what you can and can't acquire. I can put your body in chains and still not take away one iota of your freedom, as long as your freedom is in relationship to the Universe. As long as you realize that the whole totality is there, I can guarantee you that the chains won't last very long—even in a mundane, physical sense.

You chain yourself, you hold yourself back, and you refuse to understand the very simple and basic law. It's really very basic and very simple because you see it happening every day of your life. If you take a car and drive it twenty miles per hour, it takes you X number of minutes to go from point A to point B. That's cause and effect. If you drive it seventy miles per hour, it takes you fewer minutes. That's cause and effect. It's obvious to you that as you exert certain pressures in one area, you're going to get like results. So why not take it off of the mundane level and get away from the direct concerns of paying the rent, getting along with a person, or painting a picture? Simply consider this in its larger terms. Whatever you're doing is allowing the Universe to do what It does best: to give you everything you want in relationship to the degree to which you exert energy. The only thing that holds you back in human terms is being too lazy. People simply don't want to make the effort, and the Universe isn't going to make the effort for you. There are times when you say that you don't want to do something simply because you don't want to do it. Whatever excuse you use, it simply comes down to laziness. It has nothing to do with age, stamina, health, money, or anything else. It has to do only with the degree of energy you want to exert.

Some people are physically stronger than others. Some people can work eighteen hours a day and others can work only two hours. It doesn't make any difference. If you're determined to work two hours, give those two hours <u>everything</u> you've got, and the Universe will give back four more hours of return on your energy. That's exactly how you have to judge what you do—not whether someone else works eight hours and you work two or that they work two hours and you work eight. You don't worry about what the next guy is getting or not getting. You focus on the law as you know it, and the law says, "I will not defeat you. I will not desert you. I will not do anything you do not want ME to do." The Universe will never change your efforts. It will never defeat your efforts. It will never modify your efforts. If this isn't just pure undiluted strength, I don't know what is. With such strength, mountains can be torn down.

And there was evening and there was morning, the fifth day.

Genesis 1:23

Think about the meaning of the pulsation of life that has happened in this fifth day. What's produced by magnification? E N E R G Y! When looking at the number 5, you're looking at the release of energy in operation. In terms of the Story of Infinity, the fifth day is energy, which includes changes. As the earth brings forth from its kind and the Universe magnifies what issues forth, you find out where you are. Changes are produced by magnification. You go onward because of the pulsation, the accordion-like movement of life that takes place. Your life events get greater because of magnification. Changes occur because energy never stands still. Everything is constantly in motion.

The number 5 has its fingers in every pie of life. You can't turn to any incident in life without seeing 5 in action. It's the very energizing power behind all things. It is life in its own right. It is the process of expansion and contraction in its own right. In terms of the total magnitude of the numerical spectrum, 5 is, beyond a doubt, the Great Initiator. You will always find the energy of 5 within the whole concept of the beginning in anything and everything.

The number 5 is the peak number on this 10-unit plane. The mid-point between 1 and 10 is 5. If you talk about life, earth, power, and everything that you do, you can always uncover an action of 5, the action of energy within the action. Even death is a release of energy. That's why, on this earth plane, you can't have a vacuum. It just can't be because the Universe is not without the energy.

Then God said, Let the earth bring forth living creatures after their kind, cattle, and creeping things, and beasts of the earth after their kind; and it was so.

Genesis 1:24

The Story of Infinity is a large-scope activity of explaining the world. The mystical writers are distilling a volume of wisdom into the smallest conceivable word or group of words, which is an enormous task. Like all specialists, the writers will usually deal with just one subject. The preceding writer dealt with the life force mandate, and the writer before that dealt with the construction of the planet. You now have a writer who's giving you a new code indicated by the word *Then*. He is establishing that there is a repetition of the story, which tells you he's going to get down to the physical nitty-gritty.

Up to now, the other two phases have been the story of life's interaction using symbols to indicate how natural progression occurs. A new mystical writer comes along, and we have this: *Let the earth bring forth living creatures after their kind.* The word *living* hasn't been used nor could it be used before because life energy wasn't established until the fifth day. Now, we have *living creatures after their kind, cattle, and creeping things, and beasts of the earth after their kind.* What a big difference there is from *sea monsters* to these finite elements of life that are actually manifesting as *beasts of the earth,* not as *sea monsters.*

You can see that the writer is now going to take the same things that we've been dealing with in the upper levels and tell us a story about how this all works on the very lowest levels. We're now getting down to finite manifestation. Expectation is what you should have at this point.

And God made the beasts of the earth after their kind, and the cattle after their kind, and everything that creeps upon the earth after its kind; and God saw that it was good.

Genesis 1:25

The key word is *made* because God has not *made* anything up to this point. What does *made the beasts* mean? The writer has to be telling us about finite interaction on the physical levels because he's definitely not referring to higher action. He sets this up by saying, *And God made*, which is a brand new phrase. Does God make anything? No! Everything has been manifested already in terms of First Cause, so we know that he isn't telling us about God making anything. Who does the making? It is the *beasts* and the animals *after their kind* that we're concerned with here. They start interacting at a very basic level of intercourse so that they can reproduce themselves and multiply. In terms of the continuity of action, this represents the normal, regenerative process on the physical level. This is mighty significant, and all this is going on without humans having shown up yet. That's a really important point also. In contemporary religious rhetoric, you are almost always led to believe that humans show up, and then all these other things show up afterwards. It's as if mankind waved a magic wand. But, mankind hasn't even appeared yet. We have the planet, we have a life interaction, we have creatures reproducing themselves, and humans still aren't on the scene. It's terribly important for you to understand this sequence. This is why the nature kingdom (although responsive to humans) has some special, private controls all its own. Nature came first and has a direct line to the Universe.

Then God said, Let us make man in our image, after our likeness; and let them have dominion over the fish of the sea, and over the fowl of the air, and over the cattle, and over all the wild beasts of the earth, and over every creeping thing that creeps upon the earth.

Genesis 1:26

Then indicates yet another new writer, and this has to be one of the most exciting verses in the whole chapter. It's the arrival of mankind, and it has such a great deal in it. *Let <u>us</u> make man.* Since the fifth century, when the generally accepted modern Bible was produced through the Greeks, every conceivable religion with ties to Christianity has believed that mankind was made in a singular vein directly from God. It has been completely ignored that the statement reads, *Let us* [plural] *make man.* At this particular point, we have to ask who is *us*? It is so dramatic because, up to now, we can accept the Universe, we can accept that *God* means a point of consciousness focused down into an action, and we can accept a lot of things without too much traumatic action. But, when we come to this, we have no previous idea of how to define *us*.

The whole span of understanding lies right here. It's obvious that mankind was the result of more than one singular line of action. The manifestation of mankind was the result of a multiple line of action. One of the first (and only) things that you know at this point is that there must be a multiple Source. You can reason that that cannot be true because the Universe is One, and everything comes out of that One, so there's no multiplicity. However we're not talking about the Universe. We've already established that the preceding writer has brought the Story of Infinity down to a manifested level. Therefore, he isn't talking about anything in high universal terms.

The only thing to say about *us* is that *us* represents some multiple Source, as in plurality. This completely disproves any concept that suggests we have a direct lineage between God and mankind. As you well know, the whole of Christianity is based on a direct line from God to God's human son, Jesus. In the Bible, which is the very book used to promote this philosophy, we read *us*. We must know that *us* means plurality.

Let us make man in our image. Here again, the writer has made sure, with the use of *our*, that there's no question left in your mind about multiplicity. This reads like a mystery story. It's beginning to unravel some pieces, each more fascinating than the other. First of all you know, with the use of *us*, that mankind must have some multiple Source. Then, because of *our*, you know that multiple Source must have some identification. You don't know what *our* means, but you do know that there's some identification possible because of the word *image*. At this point then, you know that mankind has some identification that can be determined.

Since mankind comes from multiple Source, multiple Source must have some form of identification that can be determined through some kind of finitude by observation. This much we have been told. What else have we been told?

Let us make man in our image, after our likeness. The writer is making sure that you understand multiple Source. He used *image*, and now he's using *likeness*. This is the second time that he has used a means of identification in terms of telling us that identification can be determined. We have *image* and we have *likeness*. When we have an image and a likeness, what do we have? Look at how the word *image* has been used before.

Whatever this multiple Source is, It can identify Itself, and It does reflect. One thing we picked up along the way, without even identifying the Source, is that mankind must absolutely be a reflection. The Story tells us that we are going to *make man in our image*. Nothing can be reflected unless you have an image. Therefore, if Source has determined that mankind will be made in the *image* and *likeness*, the Source must have the ability to reflect an image. And, if mankind is made in the likeness of that Source, then mankind must be a reflection of that Source. This tells us a lot! We don't yet know what that Source is, but we do know that we didn't just manifest out of some whim.

Up to now, everything that's preceded this has been natural progression: the Universe acting and reacting to earth with everything beginning to follow a natural progression. Now, we have an indication that the universal action in universal terms (the spiritual and mental energy) is most likely complete. There is very definite action taking place here but not necessarily connected to the universal scheme of things. The universal scheme has already been laid out. The blueprint is locked in. It's now starting to build. Mankind, which is certainly on this line, is still subject to a very defined multiple Source action, one that defines Itself. It identifies Itself, determines Itself, and has a reflection. That completely throws the God-Son-man theory out the window. We cannot live with that theory at this point. There isn't any way we can live with that when *us* and *our* clearly indicate plurality as the basis of identification. If you've read all the information that has ever been printed in terms of God identification, it tells you that there's a singular theory about God; however, that singular theory just cannot live.

Let us make man in our image, after our likeness; and let them *have dominion.* Not only has the mystical writer indicated that there is multiple Source from which man manifested, but he now tells you that no matter what, there was no such thing as Adam; *them* is multiple not singular. The initial manifestation of mankind on this planet occurred in more than one. Mankind came out of multiple Source in a multiple way, so in terms of *them, man* means many.

And let them have dominion. You understand that *let* means by natural progression of the law. However, what is *dominion*? Whenever you think of the word *dominion*, I'd like you to always think of a king or a monarch who is ruling a country. This king is a king, in every sense of the word, who is intelligent and benevolent. By the grace of his people, he is given dominion over his country and over all the people in his country. This carries an enormous responsibility with it for the welfare and good of those people concerned and for the operation of his whole country. A true king would live this way. Do not ever take *dominion* out of this context. *Let them have dominion* means (in the natural progression of the law, which mankind is recipient to) that they must rule with the attendant responsibility that pertains to being rulers. Within that responsibility are all the finer aspects that attend to being a ruler. The average person simply will not face the responsibilities to the planet with dominion. It isn't assumed correctly, administered correctly, nor accepted correctly as part of the inherent responsibility. We are kings. We are queens. Therefore, dominion over Planet Earth, our current home, is our individual responsibility.

And let them have dominion over the fish of the sea, and over the fowl of the air, and over the cattle, and over all the wild beasts of the earth, and over every creeping thing that creeps upon the earth. Nothing is left out in terms of observable and manifested life. Mankind is allowed to have dominion over everything as the natural progression of manifestation. However, manifestation is not yet finished.

So God created man in his own image, in the image of God he created him; male and female he created them.

Genesis 1:27

We have not found the word *so* anywhere else up to now. It's a brand new connector. In the terms of the whole scheme of manifestation, there can't be anything added to *so*. There it is. The whole universal plan is already laid out for us, and there is no more natural progression. However, we have *So God <u>created</u>*. This is the third time that the word *created* has been used. What does that tell us? Let's go back to First Cause where everything was created in the very first verse of the story. We're getting singular again. *God created man <u>in his own image</u>*. Why the change from multiple Source to singular? We can't go on from here until we go back and identify multiple Source because we can't arbitrarily accept progression that doesn't fit mystical terms. What is multiple Source? What *image* and *likeness* manifested as mankind?

The Universe produces Its natural Master Plan in a multitude of ways, but It cannot produce mankind. The Universe is not going to produce Its parts in that sense. It goes through all the things that we just went through prior to man manifesting. Therefore, man cannot be a direct, singular projection out of the Universe. The Universe is not manufacturing Its parts on that basis of awareness. Someone has got to be doing this. Who is it? There are other parts in the Universe that continue the universal energy progression of beginning, separation, creation, organization, and energy. Those are identifiable parts with an image. Those parts can reflect themselves and see their images in their likenesses. Whatever those parts may be, they have determined to enter into the action of this planet, which is now an infant planet with nothing on it but universal energy. The parts said, in effect, that it's now time to put working consciousness into manifested form to take dominion.

The planet can't be left alone. Nothing in the Universe is left alone or void because, in the progression of the Master Plan, all things must follow, and all things must have the appropriate output. So the parts, themselves, determined to make mankind—to actually form and manifest mankind. They were not making consciousness. In effect, they were saying, "Alright. What's the most logical thing to do to make something manifest in an area that's brand new and, for all intents and purposes, virgin?" You draw upon that which you already know, that which you already imaged, and that which you had a likeness for as an expression of yourself. The only thing you can ever manifest clearly is an expression of you.

We've already read: *Let us make man in our image, after our likeness*. Stop here and recognize that that alone is absolutely stunning for two reasons. First, it took a group of them to make mankind, and second, we must have someone out in the Universe who doesn't look too very different from us. That's not an exactitude or a repetition, but it is an image and a likeness. We are look-alikes, but we're not exactly the same. They limited their job by saying, *Let us make man in our image, after our likeness*, and immediately, they limited their control by saying, *and let them have dominion*. In other words, their job was finished. They produced consciousness from the non-physical state to the physically manifested state, and now because of will, mankind can do its own thing. This is something that we don't normally consider, but we cannot escape the story.

The words *image* and *likeness* and *our* cannot imply the Universe. The Universe doesn't have an image and a likeness of Itself. It only has Itself. Reflection is on a magnitude beyond the finite form, so image and likeness must come from another finite form. Therefore, this opens up a whole bag of possibilities and considerations ad infinitum. Do we have sister planets or sister beings in some similar form or another? We aren't carbon copies because nothing in the Universe is repetitious. Are we not part of a larger family? This is extremely important. If you keep tracing along this line, you'll find the true meaning (in terms of universal unity) beyond that which you dare to dream. What you will find are very finite points of relationship: molecules to molecules, image to image, likeness to likeness, and all of this just begins to expand your awareness beyond what you ever thought possible.

To make sure that we understand what we've covered up to now, let's do a recapitulation: The Universe, in Its natural progression and outworkings, sets up the place for this planet in space. It brings the planet into being and divides the planet according to its needs with water, sky, and land. The Universe then brings forth, out if Its spirituality and out of Its own energy, the interaction of life. At that particular point, the planet (having had its breath spanked into it) determines that it will maintain itself through its own interaction of life. This interaction must be administered, like a doctor in attendance. Therefore, some beings from a similar solar system or planetary position said, "We're in a position to add our like-contribution to this new baby planet. We're going to clothe it by taking the consciousness of the planet and bringing manifestation in the form of mankind, in *our image* and *in our likeness*. Having done this, we now leave the planet to its own will and devices to *let* it take dominion and grow into its own manifestation."

This is the Story of Infinity.

Discussion Questions

Does *approval* mean the same thing as *judgment*?

What is the significance of a mandate?

What is the only thing, in human terms, that holds you back?

What is the esoteric meaning of the number 5?

How is the planet administered?

How do you expand awareness?

What does *bless* indicate?

Why can't you get something for nothing?

How do you become more satisfied with who and what you are?

How do we know, for certain, that humanity is a reflection of multiple Source?

SIX

Dominion

So God created man in his own image, in the image of God he created him; male and female he created them.

Genesis 1:27

Every planet has consciousness assigned to it from the initial universal energy that magnifies the consciousness just as we've learned is true on Planet Earth. Since the Universe cannot stop anything, this action and reaction are going on elsewhere all of the time throughout eternity. However, all we've been told, so far, is how man manifested here. The only thing that the mystical writers have told us up to this point is that some multiple Source, which is also manifested somewhere in the universe, made us in Its image and likeness. Then, through Its knowledge, Its intelligence, Its power, Its ability to separate, to create, to organize, and to energize, multiple Source turned us loose. This established free will.

In all honesty, you've always known this story. When you made a choice, in consciousness, to use Planet Earth as your current "classroom," you were given the whole Story of Infinity with nothing left out. From that point on you know, and you can't not know. It's probably the whole reason that life has become an overwhelming and incompetent disaster. You know what you're seeing and hearing is not right. Science, religion, various philosophies, and man-made laws keep painting black over your glasses, so that you can't see what you know to be true. If you take off your glasses long enough, you'll see what you absolutely know to be true.

I can tell you something that's not beyond the realm of possibilities if you want to stretch to a larger magnitude. The earth has a moon, and as far as we know, the moon is sterile and void in terms of a life force like ours. Now that we have the ability to arrive at the moon and establish a moon base, what would happen in that atmosphere and at that particular point of consciousness if we started to develop a growth process like the amoeba or the simple plant concept or the simple tadpole concept that we have here? Added to that, in terms of billions of years of maintenance, we found that we could produce an image and a likeness on the moon in terms of real manifested life because the wiser we became, the better our technology or the better our consciousness became, and we found we could do it. I'm telling you that it can be done, but I doubt seriously from my own investigation that we are manifesting anything outside of our planet at this point. We've hardly manifested on our own planet, nor have we taken dominion. We must fulfill the command of dominion because the king must take care of his own kingdom before he can go off and take care of another kingdom, and we're a far cry from that.

We've identified the Source, and we know that It's very much like we are. We know that It is intelligent and that It manifested us in Its image and likeness and then left us with dominion, which means free will. That is as it should be.

We now know what *created* means and what *so* means. However, in order to understand this, we have to go back to where we were when we first considered the reflection of God. Mankind has already manifested, by reflection, so this can't mean creation. Therefore, since creation has already been established, *created* in this case tells us that now the Universe has picked up a continuum. Our benefactors, whomever they might be, brought us into manifestation and as soon as that happened (which could have occurred very quickly or very slowly), they left us alone to take dominion. We are part of the pulsation of the earth, just as the baby who has taken its first breath. We are now breathing on our own. We don't have an umbilical chord anymore. It has been cut.

In God's image, mankind was created, *in the image of God he created him*. You know *image* to originally mean "spiritual reflection." Therefore, God's image is the image of spirituality. In other words, the physically manifested form is the image of mankind's spirituality through its phases. God didn't create mankind. God created Himself. This is a very beautiful play on words. *God created man in his own image, in the image of God he created him.* He created Himself by reflection. I reflect off of you and create me. What I see reflected from you is me, and I create myself. By whatever that image is, I am created. I reflect off of you, and I therefore create my spirituality by simply matching it up with that universal form of spirituality that I can recognize. This is the whole concept of individuality coming into the picture.

Then, *male and female he created them.* This doesn't mean that God created male and female. The writer is telling you in this business of reflection that mankind reflects their polarity. I look at you, but I don't see you. I see a reflection of me, which is the opposite polarity of my position here. You show me a polarity, whether it's the plus polarity or the minus polarity. I don't really care. At the moment that I'm looking at you and getting my reflection, I'm getting a reflection from the other polarity because I would have to. I have point A and I have point B; they represent two different points. In the reflection back, one is plus and the other is minus, whatever the situation may be.

As I see you, I'm receptive because I'm looking at an image, so you're acting as my positive polarity. I am my receptive polarity because I'm taking an image back in. In taking it back in, I relate to universal spirituality, and I now have two polarities from which to create myself. Hopefully, I create myself as a better person, but I certainly create something within myself. There you have the story of mankind's duality in form and individuality. This is how mankind came into being and how mankind found its being on a finite individual point.

None of this is given its correct interpretation or acceptance because we hate to think that there is something more intelligent or more creative than we are that exists somewhere else. In terms of mankind's mass consciousness, this is ego aggrandizement. We resent this like the animals in the forest that declare their own territory and refuse to let anyone else get into it. We've made ours, so to speak, and we just refuse to see that others are making theirs or that they can share what we have. It's really a concept of ignorance, which is even more dramatic on a planet that has been in existence for 8½ billion years. This is how far we've come, which is hardly very far. Until we can get back to the concept of our Source, to our dominion, and to the formation of the planet in line with the universal progressive plan, we're not going to get very far. We are not necessarily regressing, but without any forward movement, that could appear to be the case.

Remember, spiritual does not have an image other than spiritual. In this part of the Story of Infinity, we are talking about manifestation. Spirit only reflects spirit because it's non-physical. We needed mankind's basic Source to reflect mankind.

And God blessed them, and God said to them, Be fruitful, and multiply, and fill the earth, and subdue it; and have dominion over the fish of the sea, and over the fowl of the air, and over the cattle, and over all the wild beasts that move upon the earth.

Genesis 1:28

This is the second time that we've read that *God blessed them*. There was approval for multiplicity because it is *them* not "him." And, there was approval of the next outpouring of Universal Consciousness through all of Its definitions. *And God said to them, Be fruitful, and multiply, and fill the earth and subdue it*.

We know that God recognized, made His analysis, and approved or blessed what had been done. Then He said, *Be fruitful and multiply*. Since that has already been said once, it is a restatement of law at the physical level. This statement was at the spiritual level before, so this lets us know that the law is unchangeable. What's true at the top is going to be true at the bottom. Next we have, *fill the earth, and subdue it*. We need a definition in terms of what the writer is trying to tell us when mankind was told to subdue the earth. What was mankind given? Mankind was given dominion. Mankind is the king, and the king must control the commerce of his land in terms of the establishment of its laws, its commerce, and its goods for import and export. To *subdue* does not mean to "beat down." It means "to control and to give organization a reason for being." If you grew nothing but apples on your land, you're not going to keep everyone healthy. You need to plant other foods and have some means of control for the good of all concerned. You let some people sleep when they should sleep, putting controls in place so the noise is abated. To exercise control is part of your dominion. To *subdue* your kingdom is a magnification of the meaning of *dominion*.

Be fruitful, and multiply indicates that Universal Consciousness, First Cause, is working on all three planes: the spiritual, the mental, and the physical. In other words, energy is fruitful and multiplies itself. You've already learned, in the fifth day, that this doesn't mean having fifteen children. It does mean that you are meant to remain active. *Be fruitful, and multiply* your creativity.

The earth creates. The Universe magnifies and multiples that creation and re-infuses it with greater force so that the whole cycle of life goes on. *Be fruitful, and multiply* means to continue the cycle of life. Every thought produces another couple of thoughts. It is the natural function of the mind to constantly multiply itself and to go on.

In the phrase, *and have dominion over the fish of the sea, and over the fowl of the air, and over the cattle, and over all the wild beasts that move upon the earth,* the writer is re-establishing, without leaving any doubt, that mankind has now manifested, has been given dominion to exercise control, and is to exercise dominion over all these things. There's no question that everything here is ours and our responsibility right down the line.

And God said, Behold, I have given you every herb yielding seed, which is upon the face of all the earth, and every tree which bears fruit yielding seed; to you it shall be for food.

Genesis 1:29

No matter how we look at this, all that was provided for us to eat on this planet was initially established by law to be *every herb yielding seed, which is upon the face of all the earth, and every tree which bears fruit yielding seed.* There's no mention anywhere of killing cows or chickens or catching fish. The whole food problem has been solved. Why would the writer, who is extolling a mountain of information concerning this planet, go to such lengths regarding what we are allowed to eat? There has to be a reason and a *beginning* behind this because nothing, up to this point, has led to such finite detail. The writer goes into enormous detail to provide direction. Why is it that we are to eat vegetation and not animals? Obviously, our creative multiple Source knew, in the construction of the manifested physical body in Its image and likeness, that this was the only logical way to live in terms of perfect and natural functioning.

We can say that *dominion* means that you don't kill your subjects. That's already understood, but what is the initial cause that makes this true? Why? Why? Why? The initial cause is that multiple Source made us in Its likeness and image. Obviously, our bodily function is that likeness and image as well. Consequently, It knew that, in order for us to function correctly and with all things being equal in the program, vegetation was the food for us — nothing else. We are designed to be vegetarian and not cannibalistic or anything else. The body functions to its highest degree on a vegetarian diet. The Source that set us up functioned as indicated and saw that we need to function as that as well.

I want to point out one thing so that you don't go out and do something very stupid. I did some astral research on this problem because I was taught a great deal about nutrition, and I have never seen a vegetarian who operated well. I kept finding a basic dysfunction in the system, so I posed the question of how that could be since this is the way we are designed to live. The answer comes down to something like this: As a result of hundreds of years of producing the physical body under the wrong conditions, it can no longer operate and absorb under ideal conditions by simply shutting off an omnivorous diet and starting off in another direction. It would take on the magnitude of seven generations to produce vegetarians in the eighth generation who experience pure bodily systems. In other words, the eighth generation would be clear enough to function properly as pure vegetarians. I find that a pure vegetarian diet lacks proper brain nutrients. One of the resulting dysfunctions is that the brain's electrical function fails to operate at the proper level. You just can't switch over.

It's unwise to suddenly decide that you're a strict vegetarian. You can introduce a different balance so that, over the years, you slowly change the balance of fish and meat to vegetables and fruits. You can also make different choices about the purity of the food that you eat and live accordingly. The point is that you'd be very foolish to go on a crash diet under any conditions. Choose foods that you find the purest and diminish the amount of meat and poultry by adding more vegetables over the years. That way, the balance changes, and you're bound to benefit from not going to extremes.

And to every beast of the earth, and to every fowl of the air, and to everything that creeps upon the earth, wherein there is life, I have given every green herb for food; and it was so.

Genesis 1:30

Mankind and animals are meant to eat *every green herb for food*. The only reason that animals kill other species for food or kill each other is because mankind kills. Man kills man, and animals kill animals. If man ceased to kill animals of any kind, the beasts of the forest would no longer prey upon each other. In energy terms, mankind has dominion, and dominion means all levels of expression, including consciousness. Animals would find their nutrition from the land and from nature. Of course they would be more refined animals, and grossness would certainly disappear. Animals are subject to the overall consciousness of mankind. The planet has to be without that kind of energy completely. All killing must stop worldwide for this to occur. If we used our real intelligence, we would not be in the mess we are in.

And God saw everything that he had made, and, behold, it was very good. And there was evening and there was morning, the sixth day.

Genesis 1:31

In the sixth day, mankind manifested. They were given dominion and told how to operate in terms of the continuation of the energy flow. They were told what to eat and what the animals were to eat. The essence of the sixth day was mankind manifesting, so we have to acknowledge that the manifestation of mankind is the esoteric meaning of the number 6. However, this can't mean manifestation because we already have creation. Therefore, we have to come up with something else in terms of the definition of the number 6.

Mankind appeared from undefined consciousness into defined actuality. Up until the sixth day, the word *man* hadn't appeared. Mankind appeared, was manifested, and took dominion on the sixth day. The full range of mankind is the manifested polarity of energy on the planet. The first six numbers have to do exclusively with creation and dominion. In fact, your body is the symbolic pattern for the number 6. To prove this to yourself, lie down on the floor with your arms and legs stretched out so you have a five-pointed star. The five points are your right and left legs, your right and left arms, and your head. In the center of your body is your heart, which gives you the sixth element of man. The number 6 is mankind's number.

When you move into any incarnation, you are handed one tough job. However, to understand creation (or anything else), never stray far from basics. Look to <u>see</u> the cause and effect at all times. You don't know who you are unless you identify yourself by reflection; you cannot have finite awareness without reflection. *And the Spirit of God moved upon the face of the water* (Genesis 1:2). Do not desert the basic code. The law is reflective and progressive. What happens when you have finite awareness? You define something. When mankind was conceived out of multiple Source, they were not defined because a pattern must be established in consciousness in order to produce the creative and manifested result. That is the Law of Cause and Effect. Mankind was given dominion and made in the likeness and image of God, but this did not say that there were physical bodies of substance.

What you first have is the conceptual thought in consciousness, in which bodies existed in ghostlike forms. Mankind didn't have to do anything to maintain themselves other than feed themselves through consciousness. The directive regarding food was given, but that was the natural, reflected progression of the law.

Several billion years passed from the time that mankind was created to the progression of consciousness lowering its frequency from a non-physical, roughly invisible, state to a more solid, substantial, visible state. To live on the planet in manifestation, mankind must have the same frequency as the planet. In other words, the planet's frequency and mankind's frequency must be parallel. Energy slows down from a very high frequency to one that is compatible with the planet's frequency on which mankind has dominion. It would be very hard to take dominion when everything is solid and you're not.

If you could have arrived on the planet as an observer before mankind manifested, you would have felt energy in operation. You would have observed, as far as the function of the planet was concerned, control and organization. If you had stayed around long enough, you would have observed (**slowly** but surely) high-frequency energy moving into a slower frequency — a change in the speed of molecules. Physical form develops only by means of molecules moving at a certain rate of speed. The body's growth that starts with a sperm impregnating an egg is very solid and materialistic.

Meanwhile, the Universe is moving along at a higher frequency of energy doing what It does, no matter what.

Something very interesting is that you never lose the finer frequency because the finer frequency still exists. The physical is the grosser plane, and the spiritual is the finer plane. You always have the means (with the finer frequency tied to the Universe) to increase the rate of frequency to any degree you wish. You also have the means to increase the grosser rate of frequency to a finer rate. The ability to manifest yourself in an invisible, or non-physical, state always exists within you. You can walk through walls, walk on water, levitate, or disappear because you still retain the finer rate of frequency capabilities.

Even though you need to maintain the grosser body in order to live harmoniously with the planet itself, you are not limited. This is what makes life so amazing in terms of creation. You're given an enormous amount of capabilities, which the creators themselves had. Just look at the intricacies of the physical body's functions that were included in the manifesting plan—the Master Plan of creation. Even with what knowledge we have, we still don't know how the body and brain function or how the nervous system works. We are just barely beginning to see possibilities, but we don't know how life is constructed. The point is that we are built enormously complex, even at the grosser level. Add to that the potential and the capabilities of the finer level doing whatever it wants to the grosser level, and you have a complexity that staggers the best of your imagination.

Mankind is formed by changing molecular speed. In the basic form, the only way you get back and forth from the visible to the invisible is to change molecular speed. You find a tree and chop it down. If you cut off a piece and throw it into the fire, you've changed its molecular structure. The molecules have increased their rate from what you see to what you don't see. The whole universe is molecularly constructed. This is the very essence of your being.

Being incarnate takes a huge amount of self-care and self-love. If your self-acceptance and self-kindness cannot be applied to you, then where can they be applied? You must not translate this into an emotional feeling. When you become aware of what this means, you are touching a wisdom that cannot be defined. It's beyond the physical, yet physical manifestation is part and parcel of the spiritual, mental, and physical frequencies designed for Planet Earth. It's beneath the concept of spirituality to even attempt to define the essence of love.

Nature provides an example. She concentrates on Her own pattern and ignores all issues that could be used as limits. She fulfills the reality of what IS. However, humans use free will to look for all the limitations. Consciousness will not interfere with physicality because they are opposite polarities, and polarities are not interchangeable, nor are they separated. However, both quality and responsibility are attuned to the characteristics of spirituality.

You are what you are. Accept the harmony of duality, and be willing to share both parts of yourself with yourself in equal endeavor. To energize the duality and refurbish equally produces an inward sense of energized relaxation. It's the flow between the polarities of the physical and the spiritual frequencies that rids you of the stubborn "junk," replacing it with a sense of wholeness. That's the space without color or definition that gives you a sense of centeredness. You are magnetic!

Life is designed to be a creative process. Vitality depends upon following the precepts of the six days of creation, remembering that quality is the issue. Creative talent multiplies and produces certain "seeds," so use the creative process to discover what has already been created. No one is responsible to carry your load. Although others can give you their points of reflection, the job is yours to do. You do what you do because it is yours to do. Perfection is not the issue because, if it were possible, there would be an end to infinity. Therefore, you can't have a "total" anything. Growth is an internal quality, and eventually, it does manifest and multiply. Dominion has kilowatts of power, and you are meant to use the power wisely. The more you understand how to exercise your dominion, the more harmony you experience.

The law established dominion and handed you responsibility. Every tool you could ever want or need has been provided for you. However, you will never get anywhere in the creative process as long as you are complaining. At that point, you're just delaying the ultimate. You're unwilling to act on your responsibility because it makes you different from those around you, but something deep inside of you knows that the quality of your world is equal to the investment you make in exercising your dominion. It is you who benefits by the steps you take.

Discussion Questions

What does *dominion* mean?

How must we exercise our dominion?

What is multiple Source?

How did humans manifest on Planet Earth?

How do you know that humanity is the result of more than one singular line of action?

What is the esoteric meaning of the number 6?

What does *free will* mean?

How do you create?

Does the spiritual element have an image and a likeness?

How does the whole cycle of life progress on Planet Earth?

S EVEN

Progression

Thus the heavens and the earth were finished, and all the host of them.

Genesis 2:1

We have finished with the first six days that have to do with creation and dominion.

And on the sixth day God finished his works which he had made; and he rested on the seventh day from all his works which he had made.

Genesis 2:2

So God blessed the seventh day, and sanctified it; because in it he had rested from all his works which God created and made.

Genesis 2:3

It's time for us to look at the number 7 as the culmination number because before 7 we have the beginning (1), the separation (2), the creation (3), the organization (4), the energy (5), and finally mankind (6) — which produces what? After all of this, what have we gained in six days? We have gained the wisdom of knowing. Therefore, the number 7 is the number of wisdom. While you're learning something, is it not a struggle? However, once something settles inside of you, do you rest with the knowledge that you've finally figured it out? What you have learned really means something to you. You take a deep breath, you sit down and say, "After all that, I *finally* have this where I really want it to be." You rest, only to then go on to the next cycle of learning. Now you know why God rested on the seventh day.

Once knowledge is truly gained—that is, knowledge at the level of true wisdom—you're finished. You don't go back over it. Once you've learned that 1 + 1 = 2, you've learned it. You can rest. You don't have to learn it over and over again. There are numerous ramifications to this part of the story, one of which is dealing with karma or the cause and effect of life experiences. Once learned, you don't have to repeat the same lesson, so get to work. Then, you can rest.

And so it is. We have seven days. We run into some complexity at this point because the design of this planet is on a ten-unit plane. Consequently, we have to include the numbers 8, 9, and 10, even though this is not in the Story of Infinity as told in the first chapter of Genesis. For six days you create (struggle with your knowledge), and finally you fulfill yourself as yourself. On the seventh day, wisdom is gained and you rest. What does it mean when you rest? What happens between knowledge gained, resting, and beginning something new?

After you've arrived at the point of wisdom, you take time to assimilate what you've learned. A period of time goes by; it might be minutes, weeks, hours, or it might be years. You take time to enjoy the reflection before you start another new beginning. You take a nice deep breath and say, "Ah." There is your sound, followed by a look at what you now understand. That's followed by a reflection on that which you now understand, followed by a separation because now you're a different person. You've pulled back, and you see yourself in a different light. You then become aware, and all of this takes however long it takes before you're ready to start a new beginning. To begin anew, you have the five Prime Laws of Manifestation that precede the beginning of anything: the laws of Sound, Direction, Reflection, Recognition (separation), and Finite Awareness.

If the number 8 allows cycles of time, what does the number 9 allow? Completion; 9 is the number of completion, as knowledge that has now been induced as a permanent aspect of consciousness. Whatever has been learned becomes so much a part of you that nothing is going to add to it or diminish it. You'll never struggle to make sense out of it again. You don't have to relearn anything that you've truly learned, once you've already learned it.

Having completed the learning that the number 9 brings, you can prepare for the next level up, which is 10 or 1 to the next power (1^0). This is literally taking one step up, so you're at a new beginning. The number 10 elevates to the next level because what was a new beginning has been completed, and you start at 1 as a *new* beginning. This is the natural progression for the planet, established out of all the characteristics you've learned about that are of this planet. You can observe this natural progression of ten in so many ways, both in and out of nature as we know it. The number 10 keeps showing up in many other ways also. Consider your ten fingers and ten toes or the factors of ten in having two eyes, two ears, and two nostrils.

Once they've told you how the planet was formed and how it's to be operated according to law, the mystical writers have nothing else to tell you. They always leave you with a slight cavity inside your head waiting for you to fill it in. They don't always tell you everything, but they do tell you what you need to know. They assume, if you're the intelligent mystical student that you're meant to be, that you'll look at 7 and say, "This doesn't compute with everything else that I've learned about the planet. The planet seems to be operating in units of 10, so what happened to 8, 9, and 10?" This is what happened: Once wisdom is acquired, there has to be a cycle of rest and absorption (symbolized by 8) that completes the lesson (symbolized by 9) and then prepares for the next movement up (symbolized by 10).

The whole idea for us to understand in the Story of Infinity or other esoteric writings is how the mind and the techniques of mystical writers work. Consider how enormously capable they are in distilling a great deal of wisdom into a word or a group of words. As we've discovered, this is sometimes by omission rather than by teaching in terms of what's actually there. We must also be attentive to how they mix their writings and change authors by going from symbology to practicality. We must stay constantly aware of what's going on. This is important because it teaches you how to observe and how to look for meaning. You read a statement or a group of statements, and you don't turn away. You see the need, in terms of life and in terms of awareness, to be constantly aware, curiously aware, and questioningly aware. Do not take anything for granted. Do not take my word for it, and don't even take your own word for it. What you really want to do is ask if it's right, and if it's right, ask why it's right. Keep probing and probing and probing. There are answers upon answers upon answers. Finally, this training becomes natural to you, and everything becomes clearer, brighter, and more intense.

When you train your mind to work in a certain way, you acquire a depth of understanding that makes a huge difference in your whole attitude, intentions, and actions. Learn to understand the universal laws and the operation of those laws in your daily experience. The benefits to you are infinite.

This is your Story.

Discussion Question

How is it possible that the Story of Infinity is your story and that you have always known it?

About G-Systems International

G-Systems International provides metaphysical consultations to individuals, couples, and businesses. Our founder, Gregge Tiffen (1927-2008), developed a broad range of analytical and procedural systems to evoke the very best from individuals, both personally and professionally. Gregge's mystical training included years of intense training in the Far East during the 1960s. His direct, no-nonsense approach to human energy management lives on through G-Systems' services, publications, and audio recordings.

We are headquartered in Dallas, Texas and can be reached at 972-447-9092 or online at www.G-Systems.com.

THE COLLECTED WORKS OF GREGGE TIFFEN

Life in the World Hereafter: The Journey Continues

FIRST ENCOUNTER SERIES
Into the Universe: Extraterrestrial Activity (vol. 1)
Down to Earth: Terrestrial Activity (vol. 2)
Earth and Second Earth (vol. 3)

BOOKLET-OF-THE-MONTH SERIES
Open Secrets (2011)
The Journey Continues (2010)
The Language of a Mystic (2009)
Lessons in Living (2008)
Seasonal Reflections (2007)

BOOKLETS
Thanksgiving: The Power of Prayer, How It Works
Winter Solstice: The Christmas Story

• • •

All publications are available directly from

P Systems & Associates
P.O. Box 12754
La Jolla, CA 92039

For credit card orders and detailed descriptions, visit www.P-SystemsInc.com.

For bulk orders, call toll-free: 1-888-658-0668.

www.ingramcontent.com/pod-product-compliance
Lightning Source LLC
Chambersburg PA
CBHW031253290426
44109CB00012B/566